THE
COLUMBIA RIVER
COOKBOOK

by
Joan E. Van Divort

Cover photo: The confluence of the Columbia and Wenatchee
Rivers from Ohme Gardens. Flowers by Jim Nicholson. Fish
Platter by J. Stevens. Photo by J. Lodato.

THE COLUMBIA RIVER COOKBOOK
by Joan E. Van Divort

Copyright © 1981
Second Printing 1982
by Columbia River Press,
Box 1647, Wenatchee, WA 98801
All rights reserved.

Library of Congress Catalog Card No. 8167788
Van Divort, Joan
Columbia River Cookbook

ISBN 0-939688-04-2
Published under the auspices of
Directed Media, Inc., Wenatchee, Washington.

Dedicated to the memory of my mother, Katherine,
Who taught me to respect the wisdom of nature.

And to my husband, children and grandchildren,
Who were so willingly my guinea pigs.

Acknowledgments

With appreciation and thanks to all contributors of recipes and
stories; to The Wenatchee World, Chelan PUD and Bill
Hander for photographs provided; to Ruth Allan for the
rendering of The Old Wenatchee Shipyard; and to Jake Lodato
for exceptional assistance.

Illustrated by Robilyn Robbins.

This book will lie open flat on your
countertop or range. Open to the desired
page and firmly crease the pages where
they join in the center. To change pages,
just crease again!

ABOUT THE RECIPES

The recipes in this cookbook are tried and true, some of them popular through several generations; others newer. There are "weight-conscious" dishes; inexpensive meals-in-a-pot in tune with the conservative mood of the day; as well as glamorous, more expensive party dishes. All, however, share the same common denominator. They call for the finest ingredients obtainable with the do-it-from-scratch approach. There are no processed canned soup sauces here. You can't make a silk purse out of a sow's ear, as the old saying goes.

Many of the dishes are from my mother, who believed that if you treat your body like a garbage can, that's what you'll be. She shunned all supermarket mixes, calling them dead food. "If it isn't good enough for a worm, it isn't good enough for me," she'd say.

We weren't rich by any means, but what a smorgasbord we enjoyed! Wild mushrooms, blackberries and huckleberries; freshly picked fruits and vegetables; rich milk, thick cream and home-churned butter; our own smoked hams, bacons and sausages; steaks from our own cattle; fresh eggs; delectable fried chickens who prior to demise had run freely enjoying fresh grasses and insects (our Poulets de Bresse). We took it all for granted, never dreaming until we were out in the world how fortunate we were to have enjoyed the very best of everything on the Hobart farm.

Included are recipes I collected during my years as a Navy wife in Hawaii and Guam, and during European trips, most recently a gastronomic tour of France. Included also are family recipes and the recipes of good cooks of North Central Washington, many of them workers for the betterment of their communities as well. A few are from out-of-print Columbia River Cookbooks of the early '70s. The wonderful fruits of the area are featured.

When Ann (Greer) Baker and I opened Columbia River Kitchen it was with this thought: "North Central Washington is ready for good, old-fashioned cooking". For 3 years, an average of 200 luncheon guests a day proved that this was indeed so.

All the most asked-for-recipes during that 3-year period are here, many of them developed through trial and error by the cooks and bakers of Columbia River Kitchen. As many as possible are given with the "waste not, want not" policy and short-cut restaurant methods practised in the Kitchen.

But nothing is cast in concrete. Improvise! These recipes are but guides. Please your own taste buds. Approach your cooking as Wendy Jo Pittman does when she makes her Sourdough Biscuits (Page 143). After all, our grandmothers didn't always measure. It was a pinch of this and a teacup of that. They knew what they were doing.

Happy Cooking!

TABLE OF CONTENTS

About Columbia River Cookbooks and Columbia River Kitchen . . . .

The little Columbia River Cookbooks of the early 1970s were written to help stimulate community awareness of Wenatchee's neglected Columbia riverfront and its potential. The books featured the recipes of pioneers who came to the Northwest seeking and making a better life; and of the modern-day visionaries who have striven to preserve and protect a special, unique quality of life in North Central Washington.

Columbia River Kitchen, for 3 years a non-profit invention to raise money for a sternwheeler feasibility study, became a commercial venture that still exists, although under different ownership.

This publication is an update on Columbia riverfront development between Rock Island and Rocky Reach Dams. And a memoir of the 10-year community effort, 1966 to 1976, to establish specific cultural and recreational concepts in riverfront planning.

Of course, good cooking and good eating is a part of it all! □

Restaurant changes hands but menu to stay same

One of the Wenatchee restaurant industry's most charming success stories ends Tuesday when the sale of The Columbia River Kitchens, 400 Ninth, becomes official.

Joan VanDivort and Ann Greer have sold the quaint and popular restaurant to Bill and Glenda Hander after operating it for the past three years.

Hander's father, Vic, founded Vic's Drive In, 1851 N. Wenatchee. The couple will retain the staff, including Mrs. Greer, and the menu will remain the same.

Columbia River Kitchens, at least its namesake, actually began as a fund-raising event at Mrs. VanDivort's home for Sternwheeler Park.

The next year, Mrs. Greer joined her and the fund-raiser moved to an annual booth at the Apple Valley Street Fair.

About the same time, the women — "two little old ladies in tennis shoes" is how Mrs. VanDivort puts it — formed a partnership and began turning out aprons for sale.

It was a highly successful venture and they sold all over the state. The pair even had other women sewing for them.

It was the profits from that apron business that accounted for the down payment on the old house in which the restaurant resides.

"If there is anything that's really satisfying about the whole thing it's that we transformed what was a blight, an old shack, into an attractive, functional place that people enjoy," Mrs. VanDivort said with her usual exhuberance.

While Mrs. Greer will be staying with the business, Mrs. VanDivort will not. That's not to say she won't be active. According to the contract, she can't open a similar business for three years.

In the interim she will be writing a cookbook which will include some of Columbia River Kitchens' recipes. She also plans to further her knowledge of food in general and wines in particular and will be a tour director for a fall tour of the wine valleys of France.

She may also start a cooking school.

The Columbia River Kitchen on Ninth St. in Wenatchee, Washington. Ann Greer (left) and the author at their gala Open House in March 1977.

APPETIZERS

1

APPETIZERS

Pat Rasmussen's

BOLO SALGADO (Brazilian Salty Cake) 4 Dozen

Pat teaches foreign languages and is on speaking terms with people of many nationalities. The thin, crêpe-like batter forms a cakey crust with a colorful, quiche-like filling. Delicious and different, it slices beautifully. Try it for a luncheon, brunch or party hors d'oeuvre. Pat brought this to an Enological Society wine tasting.

BATTER
- 1 Cup cornstarch
- 1 Cup flour
- 1 Tablespoon baking powder
- 1 Tablespoon salt
- 3 Eggs
- 3 Tablespoons grated Parmesan cheese
- 1 Cup vegetable oil
- 2 Cups milk

FILLING
- 2 Large onions, thinly sliced
- 3 Medium tomatoes, peeled, seeded and cut up
- 1 Medium green pepper, chopped
- 2 Tablespoons vegetable oil
- 1 Tablespoon vinegar
- 1 Teaspoon salt

Preheat oven to 400 degrees F. Butter a 9 x 13 pan.

Place all batter ingredients in a blender and mix well. Mix vegetables in a medium bowl and stir in oil, vinegar and salt.

Pour half the batter into baking pan. Cover evenly with the drained vegetables. Pour over remaining batter. Bake one hour or longer, until toothpick inserted in center comes out clean. Serve warm or cold. Cut in squares.

Alice Stojowski's

CHEESE CHILI 4 Dozen

The following delectable, puffy creation was my favorite of all the goodies served by Alice and Al at one of their festive gatherings.

- ½ Cup (1 cube) butter
- 10 Large eggs
- ½ Cup all-purpose flour
- 1 Tablespoon baking powder
- ½ Teaspoon salt
- 2 4-ounce cans chopped chilies (NOT the hot kind)
- 1 Pint cottage cheese
- 1 Pound grated Jack cheese

Preheat oven to 400 degrees F. In 9 x 13 baking pan melt the butter, coating the pan well. Beat eggs slightly. Add remaining ingredients including the melted butter. Mix lightly. Do not beat.

Bake for 15 minutes. Reduce heat to 350 degrees and continue baking for 35 or 40 minutes longer. Cool slightly before cutting into squares.

Karen Whitmore's

CHEESE-FILLED STRUDELS   4 Dozen

Karen brought this tasty goody to a North Central Washington Enological Society wine tasting.

3-4 Cups thinly sliced onions
  3 Tablespoons unsalted butter
  2 Packages (3 ounces each) cream cheese, room temperature
1½ Cups shredded Swiss cheese
  1 Teaspoon caraway seeds
  ¼ Teaspoon salt
16 Fillo or strudel leaves
  ½ Cup unsalted butter, melted

Saute onions in the 3 tablespoons butter in large skillet over medium heat, stirring frequently until onions are transparent and golden but not brown. Cool to lukewarm. Combine onions, cream cheese, Swiss cheese, caraway seeds and salt.

Brush one side of 4 of the fillo leaves lightly with part of the melted butter and stack on top of each other. Spoon ¼ of the cheese mixture along one short side of the leaves in a strip about 1 inch wide. Roll up fillo tightly to enclose filling. Tuck the ends under. Score top of roll crosswise with sharp knife, making cuts about ¼ inch deep and 1 inch apart. Brush with butter. Repeat with remaining fillo and filling, making a total of 4 rolls. Wrap each roll in plastic wrap and seal ends. Freeze up to 3 months.

To serve, heat oven to 400 degrees F. Bake on ungreased baking sheets until golden, about 20 minutes. Cut into serving pieces along the markings.

3

Nancy Goodfellow's

CHILI GUACAMOLE

If you bring this mixture to a party you'll never have to take any back home. Three platters disappeared at Nancy and Dave Dorsey's open house. Deanna deMers put together her contribution in a motel room.

1 10½-ounce can refried bean dip	1 Chopped hard-boiled egg
1 4-ounce can chopped mild chilies	½ Pint sour cream
	1 Package (1 cup) grated cheddar cheese or Mexican flavored cheddar
1 4-ounce can chopped ripe olives	1 Package tortilla chips

½ Pint carton guacamole dip (or your own version)

On large round serving dish spread bean dip in an 8" circle. Arrange over it the chilies, then the olives. Spread on the guacamole dip. Sprinkle with chopped egg. Carefully spread on the sour cream. Sprinkle with cheese. Circle arrangement with the tortilla chips.

Make your own refried bean dip and guacamole dip if you want to reduce salt and other chemicals.

GUACAMOLE DIP

2 Large ripe avocados	1 Medium tomato, diced
2 Tablespoons lime juice, or juice of ½ lemon	1 Teaspoon minced onion
	Juice of 2 garlic cloves
1 Teaspoon Worcestershire sauce	Dash of hot pepper sauce

¼ Teaspoon salt (omit if you are making for Chili Guacamole)

Cut avocados in half, remove seeds and peel. Sprinkle with lime or lemon juice. Mash with a fork. Add remaining ingredients and mix. Cover and chill for at least an hour.

COCKTAIL PIROSHKI   Makes 32

Cocktail Piroshki may be prepared in advance, cooled, wrapped and refrigerated up to 2 days. To refresh, place on baking sheet and heat in a 300 degree F. oven for 15 minutes, until crisp. OR Piroshki may be prepared up to the point of baking and then frozen. To bake, bring to room temperature and bake as directed below.

Prepare PIROSHKI PASTRY, FILLING AND GLAZE (Page 58).

Divide pastry into 4 parts. Remove one part and cover the rest with plastic to prevent drying out.

Roll out to 1/8-inch thickness and cut into 4-inch circles with cookie cutter, can or jar. Spoon 2 tablespoons filling toward one side of each round. Moisten rim with water. Overlap other half, forming a half-moon. Seal edges firmly with tines of fork. Shape with fingers to form a crescent. Place on lightly greased baking sheet. Preheat oven to 350 degrees F.

When half the dough and filling have been used, brush each Piroshki lightly with the Glaze. Sprinkle with poppy seeds and bake for 30 minutes, or until golden brown.

Prepare remainder of Piroshki while first batch is baking.

Nancy Goodfellow's

CREAM CHEESE WITH
RED PEPPER RELISH
6 cups

Nancy's famous recipe came from Janet Gellatly. Make this during pepper season and serve during Christmas in keeping with its smashing color.

Cream cheese, as many packages as desired.
RED PEPPER RELISH
Waverly Wafers, or other white wafers

Arrange cream cheese on serving tray. Pour over the Red Pepper Relish. Surround with white wafers, such as Waverly Wafers.

RED PEPPER RELISH

12 Large sweet red peppers, coarsely ground in food grinder (about 6 cups)	2 Cups white vinegar 3 Cups sugar 1 Tablespoon salt

Mix all ingredients in 4-quart kettle. Bring to boiling, reduce heat and simmer slowly 3½ hours or longer. Pour into ½-pint jars or glasses. Seal with paraffin. The consistency should be very thick. Pouring off the juice prior to cooking will reduce cooking time and help retain the jewel-like color. Janet does not recommend grinding in a food processor, as the pieces are uneven and too much juice results.

PEPPER JUICE JELLY

Don't throw out the juice—about 1¾ cups. Instead, make a jelly, pour into individual cups and serve as a salad or accompaniment to a main dish. Pour the juice into a saucepan and bring to boiling. Meanwhile, in a small bowl mix 2 tablespoons sugar and 1 tablespoon (1 envelope) gelatin. Pour the boiling juice over and stir until completely dissolved. Add 2 tablespoons or more vinegar or lemon juice and salt to taste. Cool and refrigerate until jelled.

DEVILED EGGS

Like Chili Guacamole, always the first to go at a party.

Hardboil as many eggs as needed. Drain and plunge in cold water to loosen shells. Shell and cut in half. Mix yolks with minced onion, celery and parsley; and MUSTARD MAYONNAISE (Page 45). Fill egg halves and decorate with a tiny leaf of a green herb that's available: parsley, Chinese parsley, oregano, marjoram, tarragon, etc.

Improvise with filling mixtures: deviled ham, sardines, caviar, anchovies, garlic, capers, chopped sweet pickles, fois gras, truffles, etc.

HAM POOPOOS   4 to 6 dozen

Follow recipe for HERITAGE HAM LOAF (Page 61). Make meat balls of the first mixture. Brown in butter. Simmer in HAM SAUCE for 15 minutes. Serve hot in chafing dish. Or serve cold skewered with pineapple cubes and squares of green pepper.

LITTLE PIZZAS   2 to 3 dozen

A great favorite with Columbia River Kitchen's catered buffets. Not as much trouble as it looks if some of the components are prepared in advance. You may feel it's all worth while when you observe the popularity of these little cuties. The following recipe makes one full-sized pizza 13 inches in diameter. The dough makes a good loaf of bread.

PIZZA DOUGH

1 Cup warm water	½ Teaspoon sugar
1 Tablespoon (1 envelope) dry yeast	½ Teaspoon salt
2½ Cups unbleached all-purpose flour	2 Tablespoons vegetable oil

PIZZA SAUCE (may be prepared in advance)

2 Cups pureed tomatoes	1 Teaspoon minced fresh
1 Tablespoon olive oil	oregano or basil,
½ Teaspoon salt	or ½ teaspoon, dried
Few grindings black pepper	1 Garlic clove, minced

In a saucepan combine all ingredients. Bring to boiling, reduce heat and simmer uncovered for 30 minutes.

FILLING AND TOPPING

1 Tablespoon olive oil
2 Cups grated Romano or
Parmesan cheese
Green pepper, seeded and
sliced into slivers
Italian sausage and/or
pepperoni, thinly sliced

Lasagna Meat Sauce
(Page 94)
Anchovies
Onions, thinly sliced
Black or green olives, or
sliced, stuffed green olives
½ Pound shredded
cheese

For the dough, sprinkle yeast into water and let stand until yeast foams and bubbles up. Place flour, sugar and salt in medium mixing bowl. Make a well in the center and pour in the yeast mixture and oil. Stir together until it is well mixed and forms a ball. Turn out on lightly floured board and knead until springy. If it is sticky, add a little more flour. Place dough in buttered or oiled bowl, cover with a damp towel and allow to rise in a warm place until doubled in bulk.

Remove dough to a lightly floured surface and roll out to about 1/8-inch thickness. Cut out in 3 or 4-inch circles, using can or jar if you do not have a cookie cutter this size. Pinch edges of dough up to form rims, place on lightly oiled baking sheet and prick each one all over with a fork.

To assemble, brush each pizza with olive oil and spread with Pizza Sauce. Sprinkle with Romano or Parmesan cheese. Arrange filling ingredients of your choice in artistic designs. Sprinkle with Mozzarella cheese. Bake in preheated 400 degree F. oven for 25 to 30 minutes, or until dough is baked, and pizzas are a lovely, golden brown color. Serve immediately.

LONDON BROIL   3 or 4 dozen servings

This also a good luncheon, brunch or supper dish. See Main Dishes, Beef (Page 56).

1 Flank steak, 1½ to 2 pounds

MARINADE

½ Cup vegetable oil
¼ Cup red Burgundy wine
¼ Cup soy sauce
1 Tablespoon
Worcestershire sauce

1 Bay leaf
½ Teaspoon dry mustard
Few grindings black pepper
Dash each cayenne and
ground cloves

Score steak on both sides with sharp knife, making cuts lengthwise and crosswise of steak just deep enough to break the surface. Combine all other ingredients. Place steak in plastic bag. Pour in the marinade. Secure top tightly to prevent leakage. Place on platter and refrigerate overnight, turning occasionally.

Remove meat from marinade, drain and place on broiler rack 4 or 5 inches from heat. Broil 5 minutes on each side. Do not overcook, or it will be tough. Slice steak diagonally in paper-thin slices, slanting knife almost horizontally with cutting board.

Serve with thin slices of buttered, toasted French bread. Marinade is reusable. Strain, refrigerate or freeze.

Carol Radewan's

PICKLED MUSHROOMS

We used this recipe for many of Columbia River Kitchen's catered events, buying a lug of mushrooms at a time. You'll find that it's one of the fastest disappearing appetizers on the buffet table.

3 Cups large, whole, canned mushrooms, drained, or about a pound of fresh mushrooms, medium size.
¼ Cup olive oil
¾ Cup other vegetable oil
¼ Cup lemon juice
¼ Cup apple cider vinegar
1 Medium onion, thinly sliced
1 Teaspoon salt
¼ Teaspoon pepper
½ Teaspoon dry mustard
3 Bay leaves
½ Cup minced parsley

If you are using canned mushrooms, drain them. If fresh, remove stems and use in mushroom soup, lasagna sauce or other dish. Place in large bowl and cover with boiling water. Allow to stand 5 minutes. Drain, reserving water for stockpot.

Mix remaining ingredients except parsley. Pour over mushrooms and marinate at least 24 hours. When ready to serve, spoon into glass bowl with some of the liquid. Sprinkle with minced parsley.

Marinade is reusable. Refrigerate or freeze.

See also STUFFED MUSHROOMS (Page 123).

SASHIMI

A fresh fish. appetizer invented by Chef Yves Menoret of Bagwell's 2424, Honolulu, represented Hawaii at President-elect Reagan's pre-inaugural "Taste of America" extravaganza. This creation was a mixture of cubed Ahi (yellow fin tuna), Mahimahi (dolphin) and Opakapaka (blue snapper) laced with a dressing of mayonnaise, soy and other seasonings.

One of the joys of Hawaiian markets is the lavish display of freshly caught fish. Throw caution to the winds and experiment with the ones you or the family fishermen bring home. Delicious!

1 **Pound absolutely fresh halibut, snapper, mahimahi, swordfish, rockfish or other fresh fish**

MUSTARD-SOY SAUCE

2 **Tablespoons hot dry mustard, or Wasabi powder (Japanese horseradish)**
2 **Tablespoons hot water**
½ **Cup soy sauce**

1 **Teaspoon sugar**
¼ **Teaspoon grated fresh ginger**
Grated Japanese daikon or white icicle radish

If you are starting from scratch, skin and bone the fish. Cut across the grain into neat slices about 1/8-inch thick, or thinner if you wish. Refrigerate. Mix dry mustard or Wasabi powder with hot water. Add remaining ingredients. Chill. To serve, arrange fish on a plate on a bed of greens. To eat, dip into Mustard-Soy Sauce.

STEAMED MEAT DUMPLINGS (Siu Mai) Makes 40

Pat Kealoha instructed a class in Chinese cookery in her Red Rose Cooking School. The meat dumplings were delicious. Try this and be the star at the next party. Dumplings may be frozen and reheated.

3 **Dried mushrooms**
1 **Cup boiling water**
¼ **Cup cornstarch**
1 **Pound lean ground pork**
½ **Cup water chestnuts, finely chopped**
¼ **Cup minced green onion**
2 **Tablespoons light soy sauce, or more, to taste**

2 **Tablespoons sugar**
1 **Tablespoon grated fresh ginger**
1 **Tablespoon sherry**
½ **Teaspoon sesame oil**
¼ **Cup minced Chinese parsley (cilantro)**
1 **Package (10-ounce) round won ton skins**

9

Soak mushrooms in boiling water until softened, about 15 minutes. Chop mushrooms finely and add with ¼ cup of the mushroom water to all remaining ingredients except the won ton skins.

If you cannot find round won ton skins, round the corners of the square ones, to form circles. Place a teaspoonful of the filling in the center of each skin. With thumb and forefinger bring up the sides. Give the dumpling a turn and repeat, leaving the top open. Gather once more to form pleats and press down lightly to flatten bottom so that the dumpling will stand upright.

Arrange dumplings in round cake pans. Pour water in bottom of wok, and set the cake pan on the rack. Cover and steam 15 minutes. OR steam on a rack in a dutch oven.

Serve hot as is or with a dip of ½ soy sauce and ½ sherry wine with a few gratings of fresh ginger root.

Aileen Ramsey's

SWEET AND SOUR MEATBALLS   4 Dozen

4 Pounds pork sausage	**2 Teaspoons ground sage**
1½ Cups dry bread crumbs	**2 Tablespoons butter**
4 Eggs, lightly beaten	

Mix all ingredients except butter. Form into small balls and brown slowly in butter on all sides.

SAUCE

1 10½-ounce can beef bouillon	1 Teaspoon salt
1 20-ounce can pineapple chunks and juice	½ Cup finely chopped green pepper
1 Cup sugar	¾ Cup wine vinegar
2 Tablespoons soy sauce	4 Tablespoons cornstarch
1 Teaspoon Accent	¼ Cup water

Mix together all ingredients except cornstarch and water in medium saucepan. Bring to boiling. Dissolve cornstarch in water and add slowly to sauce, stirring. Simmer until clear and thick. Add meatballs and simmer ½ hour. Serve in a chafing dish.

SEAFOOD TRAY WITH COCKTAIL SAUCE

Center a tray with a zippy cocktail sauce and surround with prawns, Alaska King Crab legs, Dungeness Crab, chunks of cooked lobster, oysters in the shell, smoked salmon and pickled herring.

COCKTAIL SAUCE

1 Cup chili sauce
½ Cup catsup
3 Tablespoons grated horseradish
2 Tablespoons fresh lemon juice

2 Teaspoons Worcestershire sauce
3 Dashes hot pepper sauce

Mix and chill. The CHILI SAUCE in the Relishes and Accompaniments section is perfect in this sauce.

RAW OYSTERS ON THE HALF SHELL

Serve 3 fresh oysters or more per person in the shell. Spoon on Cocktail Sauce. Serve chilled, with a thin slice of lemon.

OYSTERS CASINO (Page 80) make a good appetizer.

VEGETABLE BOUQUET

Arrange raw vegetables in a bowl of crushed ice: Cauliflowrets, turnip and zucchini slices, radish roses, carrot chunks, raw mushrooms, celery strips, broccoli flowrets, green onions, raw asparagus, etc. For the dip: GREEN GODDESS DRESSING (Page 46) or your favorite.

Sternwheelers at Wenatchee Steamboat Landing. **Pringle** *at dockside.*

SOUPS & STOCKS

You could substitute canned equivalents in these soups, but how much more flavorful and full-bodied the stocks you make yourself.

COLD SOUPS

CHICKEN STOCK SOUPS

HAM STOCK SOUPS

BEEF OR VEAL STOCK SOUPS

SEAFOOD SOUPS

VEGETARIAN SOUPS

COLD SOUPS

Florence Thorner's

COLD CUCUMBER SOUP
5 Cups

One October we spent several days in Vermont at Magic Mountain Ski Resort with the Walt Stelters as guests of Hans and Florence Thorner's. A memorable dinner was highlighted with a delicious Cucumber Soup.

2 Tablespoons butter
¼ Cup chopped onions
2 Cups diced, unpeeled cucumber
1 Cup watercress leaves
¼ Cup diced raw potato
2 Cups chicken stock
2 Sprigs parsley

½ Teaspoon salt
¼ Teaspoon white pepper
¼ Teaspoon dry mustard
1 Cup heavy cream
Chopped chives, thinly sliced cucumber and/or thinly sliced or shredded radish for garnish

Melt butter in skillet. Add chopped onion and cook until transparent. Add to soup pot with all remaining ingredients except the cream and vegetables for garnish. Bring to boiling, reduce heat and simmer until potatoes are tender. Pour into blender and liquefy, or puree by forcing through a sieve. Correct seasoning and chill.

When ready to serve add the cream. Pour into bowls. Garnish each bowl with chives, cucumber and/or radish.

GAZPACHO
6 Cups

A healthful, tomato-cucumber-green pepper combination loaded with Vitamin C. Spain's famous refreshing summer soup is known also as a "salad." Make it in the morning to serve after a hot day.

2 Stale hard rolls or 1 cup bread crumbs
5 Medium ripe tomatoes, peeled
1 Medium cucumber, peeled
1 Large green pepper, seeded
1 Medium onion, chopped

1 Clove garlic, peeled
3 Tablespoons olive oil
3 Tablespoons red wine vinegar
1 Teaspoon salt, or to taste

Soak hard rolls in water. When softened, squeeze out excess water. If breadcrumbs are used, moisten only. Place all remaining ingredients in blender and liquefy until smooth. Pour into a bowl. Stir in the bread crumbs. Taste for seasoning. Refrigerate, covered, for several hours.

When ready to serve, prepare 4 side dishes: One of cucumber, one of tomatoes, one of onions, and one of parsley. Serve with the soup in chilled bowls.

TOPPING

Cucumber, peeled and finely chopped
Fresh tomato, diced

Onions, finely chopped
Minced parsley

FRUIT SOUP

The grandchildren love this one! But a combination of fresh fruits in their juices on a hot summer day is a hit with all ages. Serve with toasted whole grain bread and slices of a nice cheese such as Port Salut or Danish Havarti.

Mix any combination of seasonal fruits such as sliced bananas, apples, melons, peaches, apricots, pears; diced pineapple and oranges; fresh strawberries, raspberries, boysenberries, blueberries, grapes; stoned cherries. The addition of canned fruits such as peaches, apricots, pears, etc., is also good. See that there is enough juice to make it "soupy". Serve in soup bowls with a sprig of fresh mint.

"Bloom where you are planted"—Ella Grasso

15

CHICKEN STOCK SOUPS

CHICKEN STOCK
One Gallon

A flavorful chicken stock is a must for a good sauce or soup. The strained stock is Chicken Consomme—an epicurean treat with the addition of minced fresh parsley, chives or dill. Add leftover rice, pasta and/or vegetables for variety.

My mother served hot chicken broth during periods of convalescence. Chicken soup is a magic elixir—a universal panacea honored by generations of mothers and grandmothers and families all over the world. Jewish and Chinese mothers swear by it. Homemade chicken stock will jell, and my mother always said that was good for the joints.

1 5-7 pound stewing or roasting chicken; or chicken parts (wings, backs, necks, etc.)	2 Stalks celery with light green tops, chopped
2 Bay leaves	2 Stalks dill or 1 teaspoon dried dill weed
1 Tablespoon peppercorns	1 Large whole onion
1 Tablespoon dried thyme leaves, or 2 tablespoons, fresh	1 Cup parsley with stems
	3 Medium carrots
	1½ Tablespoons salt
	6 Quarts cold water

Place all ingredients in large soup kettle. Bring to boiling, reduce heat and simmer gently until chicken is tender, 2 to 4 hours. If chicken parts are used simmer 1½ hours. Skim surface periodically to remove foam and scum as it rises. When chicken is tender, remove from pot and set aside. Strain stock through fine mesh sieve. Cool and refrigerate.

Remove solidified fat from top of stock and store in covered container to use in cooking. Pour stock in glass or plastic containers and refrigerate or freeze if you are not using it immediately.

Use the whole chicken pieces in CHICKEN AND DUMPLINGS, CHICKEN POT PIE, (Pages 70, 72) and other dishes. Bits of chicken from the chicken parts can be salvaged for soups, salads or sandwich fillings.

TURKEY BONE STOCK

When the last scrap of meat has been salvaged from the turkey carcass, put bones in a soup pot and follow procedure for Chicken Stock. Chop leg and thigh bones to extract maximum flavor and nutritional elements.

Grace Weis'

CANADIAN CHEESE SOUP
5 Cups

Jeanne Westerberg had us over for lunch and served this delicious soup.

½ Cup finely chopped carrots
½ Cup finely chopped celery
¼ Cup (½ cube) butter, preferably unsalted
2 Tablespoons chopped onion
6 Tablespoons all-purpose flour

2 Cups milk
2 Cups chicken stock or equivalent, canned
½ Pound sharp cheddar cheese, shredded
Minced parsley for garnish

Simmer carrots and celery in ½ cup water until tender. In top of double boiler sauté onions in butter until soft, but not brown. Add flour and blend well. Place over boiling water. Add milk and chicken stock and cook, stirring, until thickened. Add cheese and stir until blended. Add cooked vegetables and cooking water. Serve topped with parsley and accompanied with toast sticks or crackers.

HAWAIIAN CHICKEN LONG RICE
10 Cups

I learned to make this soup when I lived in Hawaii, where it was and still is a great favorite. Bean thread (long rice) is sold in the ethnic sections in all the supermarkets.

1 3-4 pound stewing chicken
6 Cups water
1 Bay leaf
Salt and pepper

1 Small package bean thread
3 Cups pureed tomatoes
½ Cup chopped green onions

Chop through leg, thigh and breast bones of cut-up chicken with a cleaver. (Don't use your bread knife—it will never be the same). Place chicken in soup pot with water, bay leaf, salt and pepper. Bring to boiling, reduce heat and simmer 3 or 4 hours, until chicken is tender. Meanwhile, soak bean thread in water to cover 30 minutes. Drain in colander. Cut threads with scissors in 3-inch lengths. When chicken is tender remove from heat. Remove chicken from soup. Discard skin and bones. Skim fat from soup. Add water to make 6 cups. Return chicken pieces to soup. Add tomatoes and bean thread, bring to boiling, reduce heat and simmer, covered for 15 minutes longer. To serve, ladle into bowls. Garnish with chopped green onions.

See also CREAM OF FRESH CARROT SOUP, NON-VEGETARIAN VERSION (Page 29).

MINESTRONE WITH PESTO SAUCE   12 Cups

A great favorite with Columbia River customers. A complete meal with whole-grain or French bread, and fresh fruit and cheese for dessert.

1 Cup Great Northern or
  white Navy beans
3 Quarts Chicken Stock (Page
  16) or equivalent, canned
1 Teaspoon salt
5 Cups finely shredded
  cabbage
2 Cups potatoes cut in
  ½-inch dice
2 Cups thinly sliced carrots
2 Cups canned tomatoes, or
  fresh tomatoes, pureed
1 Cup thinly sliced onions

¼ Cup olive oil
1 Stalk celery,
  sliced 1/8-inch thick
2 Cups zucchini,
  sliced ¼-inch thick
1 Large tomato, peeled and
  cut in ½-inch cubes
1 Clove garlic, minced
¼ Cup minced parsley
  Salt and freshly ground
  pepper to taste
1 Cup spaghetti,
  broken into pieces

Soak beans overnight in water to cover at least 4 inches. When ready to prepare soup, drain beans. Turn into 8-quart soup kettle with chicken stock and salt. Bring to boiling, reduce heat, cover and simmer 1 hour. Meanwhile, prepare vegetables. When soup has cooked 1 hour add cabbage, potatoes, carrots and tomatoes. Simmer 20 minutes longer. Heat olive oil in large skillet over medium heat. Add onion and cook until transparent. Add celery, zucchini, tomato and garlic, reduce heat and cook, stirring occasionally, for about 15 minutes. Add to soup pot with parsley and spaghetti. Simmer for 20 minutes longer. Correct seasoning. Pour in bowls. Garnish with a spoonful of Pesto Sauce.

PESTO SAUCE

¾ Cup (1½ cubes) butter,
  softened
½ Cup grated Parmesan cheese
¾ Cup minced parsley
1 Clove garlic, minced
1 Teaspoon dried basil leaves,
  or 2 teaspoons fresh

½ Teaspoon dried marjoram
  leaves, or 1 teaspoon fresh
¼ Cup olive oil
¾ Cup finely chopped
  walnuts or pine nuts.

Blend Parmesan cheese, parsley, garlic, basil and marjoram with the softened butter. Gradually blend in oil, stirring. Blend in the nuts.

"Kissing don't last: cookery do."—Meredith.

SOUP AND WINE

Wines may be added to soups in the proportions of ¼ cup to one quart of soup. Dry white wine in seafood soups; Sherry or Madeira for chicken; dry red wines for beef and game.

ONION SOUP AU GRATIN   10 Cups

This was the soup served at all Sternwheeler fund raisings and also in Columbia River Kitchen.

1 Quart boiling Chicken
  Stock (Page 16)
1 Quart boiling Beef Stock
  (Page 23)
5 Large onions, about 1½
  pounds, thinly sliced
3 Tablespoons butter

3 Tablespoons flour
¼ Cup Worcestershire sauce
  Salt and pepper to taste
  French bread rounds,
  toasted on one side
  Grated Parmesan and
  Swiss Cheese

Heat chicken and beef stocks in large soup kettle. In large skillet over medium heat cook onions in butter and oil until golden brown. Remove from heat. Stir flour into onions and blend well. Return to heat. Cook 3 minutes longer. Add a quart of the boiling stock all at once, stirring constantly, until thickened. Reduce heat and simmer 3 minutes. Add to soup pot. Add Worcestershire sauce. Taste for seasoning. Ladle into soup bowls over toasted French bread. Sprinkle with cheeses. Serve immediately.

If you wish to broil the cheeses, ladle soup into ovenproof bowls. Place untoasted French Bread on the soup, sprinkle with the cheeses and run under broiler until cheeses are bubbling and bread is golden brown.

HAM STOCK SOUPS

HAM STOCK
6 Quarts

6 Pounds smoked ham hocks, smoked ham and/or ham bones and rind
2 Gallons cold water

Place ham hocks, bones, etc. in large soup pot. Add water. Bring to boiling, reduce heat and simmer, covered, 5 or 6 hours, until meat falls off the bones. Skim surface periodically to remove foam and scum as it rises. When ready, remove hocks, bones and rind. Remove meat from hocks and bones and reserve. Discard bones, fat and rind. Strain stock thru fine mesh sieve. Cool and refrigerate. Remove solidified fat from top of stock and discard. Place stock in glass or plastic containers and refrigerate or freeze.

BASQUE LENTIL AND SAUSAGE SOUP
16 Cups

A complete meal with the addition of a green salad or raw vegetables, or fresh fruit and a whole grain roll. Leftover ham bones, bits of ham, or waters in which ham or corned beef, sausage or tongue have been cooked, may be used. But watch the salt!

2 Cups kidney beans, cooked	1 Bay leaf
2 Cups lentils	2 Cups shredded cabbage
3 Quarts Ham Stock	3 Tablespoons lemon juice
2 Tablespoons butter	3 Cups sliced, cooked Polish
2 Cups chopped onions	or German sausage
2 Cups carrots,	1 Cup ham pieces
sliced ¼-inch thick	Salt and pepper to taste
½ Cup celery with leaves*	½ Cup minced parsley
2 Cups diced potatoes	for garnish

If you are using dried kidney beans, soak 1 cup beans overnight in water to cover at least 4 inches. Drain. Rinse and drain lentils. Place lentils and beans in large soup pot with ham stock. Bring to boiling, reduce heat and simmer 2 hours. (If you are using canned kidney beans, add later with vegetables and simmer lentils only until tender).

In a frying pan over medium heat cook onions in butter until transparent. Add to soup with carrots, celery, bay leaf and kidney beans with liquid (if you using canned beans). Bring to boiling, reduce heat and simmer, covered, ½ hour. Add potatoes and simmer 20 minutes longer, until tender. Remove from heat. Discard bay leaf.

Puree 4 cups of the soup and vegetables. Return to pot. Add cabbage, lemon juice, sausage and ham. Bring to boiling, reduce heat and simmer 15 minutes longer. Season to taste. Serve with a sprinkling of chopped parsley.

*Use only the light green leaves, as the dark leaves impart a bitter taste.

BEAN SOUP   12 Cups

An old-fashioned soup said to be the favorite of the U.S. Senate Dining Room. Serve CORNBREAD (Page 147) and a green or fruit salad for a complete meal. A good bean soup requires a good, strong ham stock.

3 Cups Great Northern or Navy beans	8 Stems parsley
3 Quarts Ham Stock	2 Bay leaves
3 Tablespoons butter	1 Carrot
3 Cups chopped onion (about 4 large)	½ Lemon
1 Clove garlic, minced	2 Cups leftover ham or ham pieces from boiled ham hocks
1 Teaspoon dried thyme leaves, or 2 teaspoons fresh	Salt and pepper to taste

Place beans in a bowl and cover with at least 4 inches of cold water. Soak overnight. Drain and place in large soup pot with the ham stock. In a frying pan over medium heat melt butter, add onions and cook until transparent. Add to soup pot. Add thyme. Tie parsley, bay leaves, carrot and lemon in a cheesecloth bag and add to pot. Cover, bring to boiling, reduce heat and simmer about 3 hours, or until beans are tender. Remove and discard cheesecloth bag. Puree 4 cups of the beans and liquid. Return to pot. Add leftover ham pieces. Heat to boiling. Season to taste.

SAUERKRAUT SOUP   8 Cups

Sometimes my mother served boiled potatoes with this soup, but always rye or pumpernickel bread.

1 Smoked ham hock	1 Dill stalk or ½ teaspoon dill weed
1 Quart water, or to cover	1 Tablespoon honey
1 Large onion, thinly sliced	1 Cup whipping cream
2 Tablespoons butter	Salt and pepper to taste
1 Quart sauerkraut	
1 Tablespoon pickling spices, cloves and cinnamon removed, tied in a cheesecloth bag, or placed in a teaball	

21

Boil ham hock in water until it falls apart. Remove from stock. Discard bones, skin and fat. Reserve ham pieces. Skim fat from broth. Strain. Add enough water to make one quart. In a frying pan over medium heat cook onion in butter until transparent. Place sauerkraut in colander and rinse with tap water to remove excess sharpness. Squeeze out excess moisture and add to ham broth along with onions, spices and dill. Bring to boiling, reduce heat and simmer, covered, one hour. Remove from heat. Remove spices and dill stalk. Add honey and reserved ham. Taste for seasoning. Pour into bowls. Serve with cream.

SPLIT PEA SOUP
10 Cups

Legume soup recipes are to be found in all the old cookbooks under the headings of split pea, bean, lentil, etc. This is a soup that has endured and is as popular in homes and restaurants today as it was in the homes of 1776.

2½ Cups split peas
  3 Quarts Ham Stock
  1 Bay leaf
  2 Tablespoons butter

1 Cup chopped onions
1 Cup chopped carrots
Ham pieces (optional)

Soak peas overnight in water to cover at least 4 inches. Drain. Pour stock in soup pot. Add peas and bay leaf. Bring to boiling, reduce heat to simmering. Melt butter in skillet over medium-high heat. Add onions and carrots and cook until onions are transparent, stirring. Add to soup. Simmer 3 hours. Remove 4 cups of the soup and puree. Return to pot. Adjust seasoning to taste. Add ham pieces if desired.

BEEF OR VEAL STOCK SOUPS

BEEF OR VEAL STOCK
One Gallon

It is amazing how much more creative one can be when there is a "bank" of stocks on which to draw when a special dish, occasion or emergency demands.

4 Pounds beef or veal knucklebones	3 Stalks celery with tops
	1 Large whole onion
2 Pounds sliced beef marrowbones	1 Cup parsley with stems
	3 Carrots
3 Bay leaves	1½ Tablespoons salt
1 Tablespoon peppercorns	6 Quarts cold water
2 Cloves garlic	

Place all ingredients in large soup kettle. Bring to boiling, reduce heat and simmer gently about 4 hours. Skim surface periodically to remove foam and scum as it rises. When ready, remove bones and discard. Strain stock through fine mesh sieve. Correct seasoning. Cool and refrigerate.

Remove solidified fat from top of stock. Discard (unless you're making soap or winter food for the birds). Place stock in glass or plastic containers and refrigerate or freeze.

BROWN STOCK

Browning the bones and vegetables first adds a nice flavor and color to Beef or Veal Stock. Preheat oven to 400 degrees F. Spread bones and chopped carrots, celery and onion in roasting pan. Bake 20 to 25 minutes—not too long, or your stock will be a dark brown color. Your goal is a nice amber. Remove from oven. Add to soup pot with all remaining ingredients and follow recipe for Beef or Veal Stock

"Scum and cream both rise to the top."

CALVES' FOOT SOUP WITH POACHED EGGS

Now here's an oldie from an old-time cookbook published at the turn of the century:

Boil 2 pair of calves' feet and 1 shank of ham from which the rind has been removed in 3 quarts of water for at least two hours, add 2 sprigs of parsley, the same of thyme (kitchen herb for seasoning), a blade of mace and pepper and salt to taste. Boil two hours longer, strain and set away to cool. When cold, remove carefully all the fat and return to the kettle. The soup should be cleared by breaking in 1 egg and stirring briskly for a moment. Then as it begins to boil skim carefully or strain through a bag. Poach as many eggs as there are persons to be served, place in a tureen, pour the hot soup over them and serve at once.

VEGETABLE-BEEF SOUP WITH NOODLES 18 Cups

My mother's vegetable soup was a meal in itself with thick slices of homemade bread and home-churned butter, with home-canned peaches for dessert. Reduce ingredients for a smaller batch.

3 Quarts Beef Stock	½ Cup diced green pepper
2 Pounds lean brisket of beef, or other boiling beef	1 Cup green beans, sliced julienne
2 Cups chopped onions	2 Cups potatoes cut in ½-inch dice
2 Cups chopped celery or celeriac	1 Cup peas
2 Cups sliced carrots	1 Cup minced parsley
2 Cups cooked tomatoes, or fresh tomatoes, peeled and chopped	Salt and pepper to taste
	Cooked noodles (optional)

In large soup kettle pour beef stock. Add brisket of beef, bring to boiling, reduce heat and simmer until beef is tender, about 2½ or 3 hours. Skim off the scum as it rises to the top. Remove beef from pot. Discard fat, gristle and bone. Set meat aside. Skim fat from soup. Add water to bring to 2½ quarts.

Add onions, celery, carrots, tomatoes, green pepper, beans and potatoes to pot. Bring to boiling, reduce heat and simmer 15 minutes. Add peas and simmer 5 minutes longer. Add reserved meat, parsley and cooked and drained noodles. Simmer 5 minutes longer. Correct seasoning. Remove from heat and allow to rest for 15 minutes before serving.

Katherine's
HOMEMADE NOODLES

2 Cups unbleached all-purpose flour	3 Large eggs
½ Teaspoon salt	1 Tablespoon water, or more if needed

Sift flour and salt into a bowl. Make a well in the center and break into it the eggs. Add water. Break egg yolks with a fork and stir until dough leaves sides of bowl. Divide into 2 balls. Roll each ball out on floured surface, stretching the dough paper thin. Let stand 30 minutes, or until sheets feel dry. Roll up like a jelly roll. With sharp knife cut into very narrow strands. Toss lightly to separate strands. Boil in fast boiling salted water for 10 minutes. Drain.

VARIATIONS TO VEGETABLE-BEEF SOUP

BORSTCH: *There are hundreds of variations of Borstch. This is just one.*

Omit carrots, green pepper, beans and peas in Vegetable-Beef Soup. In saucepan cook onion and 1 clove minced garlic until onion is transparent. Add celery or celeriac, 3 cups peeled, shredded beets, 5 cups shredded cabbage, 1 bay leaf, the parsley, salt, pepper, ½ cup red wine vinegar and 1 tablespoon sugar. Cover, bring to boiling, reduce heat and simmer, covered, about 30 minutes.

Add potatoes to stock in soup pot. Bring to boiling, reduce heat and simmer until potatoes are almost tender. Add cabbage and beet mixture and simmer 20 minutes longer. Add cooked beef, correct seasoning. Serve garnished with sour cream and a sprinkling of minced parsley. Serve with PIROSHKI (Page 58), if desired.

SWEDISH MEATBALL SOUP: Substitute SWEDISH MEAT BALLS (Page 75) for brisket of beef. Add browned meat balls with peas. Omit Noodles.

VEGETARIAN VEGETABLE SOUP: Omit meat in Vegetable-Beef Soup. Substitute water or leftover vegetable waters for the beef stock. Barley, lentils, rice, spinach noodles or other pasta may be added.

25

Hotel Mundial's

SOPA PAYSANNE 5 Cups

I remember Portugal for Fado—its sad, soulful folk music—and for its wonderful soups and baskets of delicious crusty rolls and sweet cream butter.

4 Cups Beef Stock or
  equivalent, canned
  and diluted
¼ Cup *each* finely chopped
  carrot and turnip
¼ Cup finely chopped mustard
  greens, turnip greens or
  cabbage

2 Tablespoons finely chopped
  pimiento
Dash red pepper
Salt and pepper to taste
3 Tablespoons bacon fat or
  olive oil
3 Tablespoons flour

Pour stock in soup pot, add vegetables and seasonings, bring to boiling, reduce heat and simmer 10 minutes. Meanwhile, melt bacon fat or heat olive oil in skillet, blend in flour, stirring until slightly browned. Add 2 cups of the boiling stock all at once, stirring constantly until thickened. Return to soup pot, blending well. Serve at once.

Clam gunning at Ocean Shores

SEAFOOD SOUPS

BOSTON STYLE CLAM CHOWDER · 10 Cups

The Friday lunch favorite at Columbia River Kitchen. Serve with Oyster crackers, soda or Pilot crackers, or a crusty roll.

3 Slices bacon, cut fine
1 Cup chopped onions
1 Cup chopped celery
2 Cups potatoes cut in
½-inch dice
4 Cups clam nectar
1 Teaspoon fresh thyme, or
½ teaspoon dried

3 Tablespoons butter
3 Tablespoons flour
1 Quart hot milk
2 Cups minced clams
and juice
½ Cup minced parsley
Salt and pepper to taste

In skillet, fry bacon until crisp. Transfer to soup kettle using slotted spoon. Drain all fat from skillet except one tablespoon. Cook onion in bacon fat until transparent. Add to soup kettle, along with celery, potatoes, clam nectar and thyme. Bring to boiling, reduce heat and simmer, covered, until potatoes are tender. Meanwhile, melt butter in skillet and blend in the flour. Allow to bubble for 3 minutes, stirring. Pour in the hot milk all at once and whisk until thickened. Add to soup pot. Add clams and parsley. Salt and pepper to taste. Simmer 5 minutes. Serve.

MANHATTAN STYLE CLAM CHOWDER · 12 Cups

You'll meet friends from North Central Washington at Ocean Shores. Armed with "clam guns" they're after the elusive, succulent Razor Clam. These denizens of the ocean sands make a rich and delicious soup, replete with the rejuvenating minerals of the sea. A complete meal with crusty rolls or toasted French bread.

1½ Quarts water
2 Cups potatoes, cut in
½-inch dice
½ Cup chopped celery
2 Cups cooked or fresh
tomatoes, pureed
1 Teaspoon fresh thyme
leaves, or ½ teaspoon dried
2 Teaspoons salt
¼ Teaspoon pepper

8 Slices bacon, cut fine
1 Cup chopped onion
3 Tablespoons butter
3 Tablespoons flour
1 Tablespoon Worcestershire
sauce
1 Quart minced butter or
razor clams and juice.
More or less as desired
½ Cup minced parsley

If you are using fresh razor clams, remove and discard gills and digestive tract. Grind the rest. Pour the water into a large soup kettle. Add potatoes, celery, tomatoes, thyme, salt and pepper. In a skillet fry bacon until crisp, remove with slotted spoon and add to soup pot. Drain fat, leaving one tablespoon in the pan. Add onions and cook until transparent. Add to soup pot. Bring to boiling, reduce heat and simmer, covered, until potatoes are tender. Melt butter in skillet and blend in the flour.

Allow to bubble for 3 minutes, stirring. Add a quart of the hot soup all at once, whisking until thickened. Return to soup pot with Worcestershire sauce, clams and parsley. Taste for seasoning. Simmer 5 minutes. Serve.

MANHATTAN FISH CHOWDER: Substitute for the clams any one or combination of the following fish cut in 1-inch chunks: halibut, salmon, petrale sole, Greenland turbot, rex sole, lingcod, red snapper, or whatever you have caught that you like. Shelled and deveined shrimp may be added. Or lobster meat. Simmer soup 10 minutes after adding fish.

OYSTER STEW
6 Cups

Serve this comforting dish with Oyster crackers, naturally.

2 Tablespoons butter	2 Cups milk
1 Tablespoon finely minced onion	1 Cup light cream
	Salt and white pepper
1 Quart small or medium fresh oysters	Butter and paprika
	Minced parsley

In top of double boiler cook onion in butter until transparent. Remove from heat and add oysters, milk, cream, salt and pepper. Place over simmering water. Cover. When milk is hot and oysters are plump and floating, add the parsley. Place a dab of butter in each soup bowl. Ladle in the stew. Sprinkle with paprika.

VEGETARIAN SOUPS

CREAM OF FRESH CARROT SOUP   16 Cups

Popular with Columbia River Kitchen regulars, this recipe is for a large group. Just halve the ingredients for a family-size batch.

2 Quarts water
1 Teaspoon salt
¼ Teaspoon white pepper
½ Cup brown rice
7 Cups carrots cut in
   small dice
1½ Cups chopped onions

1½ Cups chopped celery
6 Tablespoons butter
6 Tablespoons flour
1 Quart hot milk
Minced parsley, chives or
   fresh dill for garnish

Place water, salt, pepper and rice in large soup kettle. Bring to boiling, reduce heat and simmer 40 minutes or until rice is tender. Add carrots, onions and celery and simmer until vegetables are tender, about 10 minutes.

Melt butter in medium saucepan, blend in the flour and allow to bubble 3 minutes, stirring. Add hot milk all at once and stir vigorously until thoroughly blended and thickened. Add to soup pot and blend. Taste for seasoning. To serve, pour into bowls and garnish with minced parsley, chives or fresh dill.

CALORIE WATCHERS' VERSION: Omit butter and flour. Ignore preceding paragraph. When vegetables are tender, measure 4 cups of the soup mixture into blender jar and puree until smooth. Return to soup pot. Add hot milk. Taste for seasoning. Pour into bowls. Garnish.

NON-VEGETARIAN VERSION: Substitute chicken stock for water.

PUREED FRESH CARROT SOUP: Puree in blender. Strain and reheat. Pour into bowls and garnish. (Cream may be added for a richer version).

CARROT VICHYSSOISE: Substitute 1 quart diced potatoes for the rice. Place in soup pot with water, salt, pepper, and vegetables. Cook until just tender. Puree in blender. Chill. Add cream for a richer soup, if desired. Pour into bowls. Garnish.

VARIATIONS TO
CREAM OF FRESH CARROT SOUP

Delicious substitutions for carrots may be made, varying only the cooking time of vegetable, and the seasoning. Following are a few suggestions:

CREAM OF ZUCCHINI, CREAM OF CAULIFLOWER, CREAM OF GREEN BEAN: Substitute appropriate vegetable for carrots.

CREAM OF FRESH SPINACH: Substitute chopped spinach leaves for carrots and add 5 minutes after onions and celery. Stir in ½ teaspoon nutmeg just before serving.

CREAM OF BROCCOLI: Cut off hard, inedible part of stalk. Substitute chopped edible stalks and the flowrets for carrots. Add 1 teaspoon ground oregano and 2 teaspoons curry powder. Garnish with thinly sliced lemon.

MORE VEGETARIAN SOUPS: Gazpacho and Fruit Soup in Cold Soup Section. Vegetarian Vegetable Soup in Beef Stock Soup Section.

Katherine's

CREAM OF POTATO SOUP
6 Cups

My childhood memories of the farm in Hobart include a parade of traveling men. Some were gatherers of seeds and barks. Some were buyers: the Rag Man and the Junk Man. Some were sellers: the Raleigh Man and the McNess Man; the peddlers of "doctor" books; bibles; encyclopedias; religious pictures; plants and seeds; dresses and aprons; pots and pans.

There were exciting times, when in return for an overnight stay or a meal, a gift would be ours. The best one of all was a Pearl Rhododendron—its glorious masses of pink bloom eventually reaching the eaves of our front porch.

One memorable peddler, a plump old gentleman whose bushy white mustache was rimmed in orange, always timed his call at noon. How he relished my mother's potato soup! After each leisurely slurped spoonful he would place a forefinger over his mustache and noisily suck in the fringes, while we kids watched in goggle-eyed fascination.

3 Cups diced potatoes, about 4 medium	3 Cups milk
½ Cup chopped onion, about 1 medium	3 Tablespoons butter, softened
½ Cup chopped celery	3 Tablespoons flour
½ Cup minced parsley	Salt and pepper to taste
1½ Cups water	Paprika for garnish

Pour water into medium saucepan. Add potatoes, onion, celery and parsley. Bring to boiling, reduce heat and simmer, covered, until potatoes are tender.

Add milk and heat. Mix softened butter and flour. Blend in liquid from the pot until thin enough to pour. Return to pot, stirring until thickened. Add salt and pepper to taste. Simmer 3 minutes. Pour into bowls. Sprinkle with paprika and minced parsley, if desired.

31

6 Cups

OLD FASHIONED CREAM OF TOMATO SOUP

My mother never added soda to her tomato soup, but told us to always pour the tomatoes into the milk (red into the white) to prevent curdling. However, I have found that some tomatoes are so high in acidity that this simply does not work. The soda is your insurance.

4 Cups rich milk
2 Cups cooked tomatoes
  Pinch of soda
4 Tablespoons butter

4 Tablespoons flour
  Salt and pepper to taste
  Chopped chives for garnish

Heat milk and tomatoes in separate pans. Heat milk until skin forms. Add soda to tomatoes. Melt butter in medium saucepan. Blend in flour and allow to bubble 3 minutes, stirring. Add scalded milk all at once and continue stirring until thickened. Remove from heat. Cool 2 or 3 minutes. Add hot tomatoes, stirring. Add seasoning to taste. Pour into bowls. Sprinkle with minced chives or green onion tops.

RUSSIAN STYLE MUSHROOM SOUP   11 Cups

Served at a Sternwheeler fund-raising, this soup was a great success.

½ Cup (1 cube) butter
4 Cups sliced fresh
  mushrooms
½ Cup chopped onions
1 Stalk celery, minced
2 Cups thinly sliced
  raw potatoes

6 Cups water
1 Cup sour cream
½ Cup minced green
  onion tops
¼ Cup minced parsley
  Chopped fresh dill
  for garnish

Melt butter in large saucepan over medium heat. Add mushrooms and cook for 3 minutes. Add onions and celery and cook, stirring, until liquid evaporates. Add potatoes and water, bring to boiling, reduce heat and simmer covered for 20 minutes. Remove from heat, allow to rest 5 minutes. Stir in sour cream, minced green onion and parsley. Pour into soup bowls. Garnish with chopped dill. *Do not boil after sour cream has been added, or soup will curdle.*

32

*Steamer **Bridgeport** on excursion. Brewster, July 2, 1928.*

Robilyn Robbins

& DRESSINGS

DRESSINGS

Ann (Greer) Baker's

CHICKEN SALAD
Serves 8

Ann's salad was much in demand for catered events during Columbia River Kitchen days. Turkey white meat may be substituted.

6 Cups diced chicken breast meat, medium dice (about 3 whole chicken breasts)

½ Cup finely diced celery, including light green tops

3 Hard-boiled eggs, diced

¼ Cup finely diced onion

3 Cups Red Delicious apples, with skins, cut in medium dice (about 3)

½ Cup diced black olives

2 Cups green seedless grapes

Place all ingredients in bowl and lightly toss with dressing just before serving.

DRESSING

1 Cup mayonnaise

¼ Cup lemon juice

1½ Teaspoon curry powder

Dash salt and pepper

Blend ingredients well.

COLE SLAW
Serves 8

4 Cups finely shredded cabbage

¼ Cup *each* grated carrot, chopped green pepper and chopped green onion

1 Teaspoon celery seeds

Combine ingredients. Toss with DIETERS' BUTTERMILK DRESSING (Page 43), BASIC FRENCH DRESSING or VARIATIONS #1 or #2 (Page 43), or GREEN GODDESS DRESSING (Page 46) with sugar added to taste, if desired.

Ann Deal's

COLE SLAW DRESSING

Add ¾ cup sugar and 10 sliced, stuffed olives to cabbage mixture. Boil together 1 cup vegetable oil, 1 cup white vinegar, 1 teaspoon salt and ½ teaspoon dry mustard. Pour over cabbage hot. Let stand in refrigerator 24 hours. Will keep a week, covered.

CRAB SALAD
Serves 6

The Palace Court of San Francisco's Palace Hotel served the most wonderful crab salad I have ever tasted. This is the way I remember it.

3 Cups fresh Dungeness crab-meat, or more, plus a few legs for garnish
1½ Cups finely diced celery
1 Tablespoon minced green onion
¾ Cup Mayonnaise (Page 45) or just enough to bind shredded lettuce

6 Large slices ripe tomato, skinned
6 Large cooked artichoke bottoms
3 Hard-cooked eggs, finely chopped
Thousand Island Dressing (Page 46)

Plunge large, ripe tomatoes in boiling water just long enough to remove skin. Peel and slice. Combine crab meat, celery, onion and mayonnaise in a bowl. Place shredded lettuce on each plate. Top with thick slice of tomato. Place an artichoke bottom on each slice of tomato and fill with the crab mixture. Wreath artichoke with a sprinkling of chopped egg. Serve with THOUSAND ISLAND DRESSING (Page 46).

VARIATIONS

TOMATO-CRAB: Plunge large, firm, ripe tomatoes in boiling water just long enough to remove skin. Remove hard stem center. Place on lettuce cups or other greens, cut into 8ths, but not all the way through, to form a half-open "flower" basis for the filling.

AVOCADO-CRAB: Another substitute for the artichoke. Use fully ripe peeled halves, sprinkle with lemon juice to prevent darkening, fill with crab mixture.

CRAB FILLING VARIATIONS: Substitute shrimp or diced, cooked chicken or turkey for crabmeat. King crab could be substituted for Dungeness.

GARNISH: Let your creativity soar. Black olives, pimiento strips, radish roses, red or green pepper strips, minced parsley or chives, watercress, pickled mushrooms, grapes, slices or wedges of lemon or lime, etc.

FRESH FRUIT SALAD

Columbia River Kitchen's Fruit Salad with Honey-Lemon Dressing was one of the most asked-for recipes. Only fresh fruits in season were used: peaches, apricots, pears, apples, melons of all kinds, oranges, grapes, bananas, strawberries and other berries in season. A meal in itself with a slice of good wholegrain bread.

HONEY-LEMON DRESSING

1 Cup fresh lemon juice	2 Teaspoons salt
2 Cups pineapple juice	1 Cup good-quality
2 Tablespoons paprika	vegetable oil
1 Tablespoon dry mustard	3 Cups honey

Combine all ingredients and blend. If mixing manually, combine juices and seasonings and gradually add oil and honey. Cover and refrigerate.

POTATO SALAD   Serves 8

Save pickle juices for your "bank" of ingredients for dressings.

8 Medium-sized potatoes	¼ Cup minced parsley
6 Large eggs	½ Cup sour cream
½ Cup Basic French Dressing	½ Cup mayonnaise
(Page 43) or more	1 Tablespoon dry
½ Cup sweet pickle or	mustard
dill pickle juice	Green pepper rings
1 Teaspoon celery seeds	Quartered tomatoes,
½ Cup minced celery	or cherry tomatoes
½ Cup minced green onions	Minced fresh dill weed
or chives	Salt and pepper to taste

Boil potatoes in their jackets along with the eggs. When potatoes are tender, drain, cool slightly, peel and dice or crumble. Run cold water over the eggs to loosen shells, then peel and chop 4 of them. Reserve remaining 2 for garnish. In a large bowl mix the potatoes, chopped eggs, French dressing, pickle juice and celery seeds. Cool and refrigerate.

When ready to serve, add celery, onion and parsley. Combine mayonnaise, sour cream and mustard. Add to salad and mix well. Taste for seasoning. Add salt and pepper and more mayonnaise and mustard if you think it necessary.

Line a bowl or platter with salad greens. Mound with the salad. Garnish with the 2 remaining sliced hard-cooked eggs, pepper rings, tomatoes, dill and whatever you like.

HOT POTATO SALAD   Serves 8

8 Medium-sized potatoes	¼ Cup minced parsley
10 Strips bacon, diced	1 Teaspoon celery or
¾ Cup Basic French Dressing	caraway seeds
(Page 43)	Salt and freshly
½ Cup minced green onion	ground pepper

Boil potatoes in their jackets. While they are cooking, saute bacon in skillet until crisp. Remove from pan with slotted spoon. Drain on paper toweling. Peel potatoes while still hot (do it with your rubber gloves) and dice or crumble into a bowl. Toss with French dressing. Mix in remaining ingredients. Taste for seasoning. Serve hot.

SPINACH SALAD   Serves 8

I have eaten Spinach Salad with all kinds of dressings: sharp, mild, creamy, even flaming.

1 Pound fresh spinach, washed, stems removed, drained	½ Small red onion, sliced in paper-thin rings (optional)
4 Hard-cooked eggs, chopped	½ Teaspoon salt
8 Slices bacon, crisply fried and crumbled	1 Clove garlic, halved
¼ Pound fresh mushrooms, cleaned and sliced	

Tear spinach leaves into bite-size pieces. Chill. Just before serving, sprinkle salt in salad bowl and rub with garlic halves. Discard garlic. Add all other ingredients to bowl. Toss with BASIC FRENCH DRESSING (Page 43) or any of the variations.

DILL WEED DRESSING
Spinach Salad is popular with patrons of River-Haven Restaurant. Here is Chef Steve Gordon's recipe.

2 Cups mayonnaise	1 Teaspoon garlic salt
1 Cup sour cream	1 Tablespoon lemon juice,
3 Heaping teaspoons	or to taste
dill weed	Light cream

Blend mayonnaise, sour cream, dill weed and garlic salt. Add lemon juice to taste, and thin to desired consistency with half and half.

SALADE NICOISE   Serves 6-8

This is a salad you'll find in the Charcuteries of France. It was on the menu when Columbia River Kitchen catered a luncheon, served on Stevens Pass, for an ALCOA theatre bus party to Seattle.

1 3½-ounce can tuna, water-packed
4 Medium or 8 small new potatoes, peeled
1 Cup julienned cooked ham*
1 Cup shredded white chicken meat
1 Cup julienned mortadella or other sausage
1 Red pepper, julienned
1 Green pepper, thinly sliced
1 Stalk celery, cut in thin, 2-inch strips

2 Large tomatoes or more, cut in quarters, or cherry tomatoes
1 Red onion, thinly sliced
4 Hard-cooked eggs, halved
1 2-ounce can anchovy fillets, drained
2 3¾-ounce cans sardines
3 Tablespoons chopped fresh herbs (parsley, basil, chives), mixed Greek olives, radish roses, curly lettuce for garnish
Salt and freshly ground pepper

Cook potatoes until tender. Cool slightly. Slice into ¼-inch thick rounds; or leave whole, if small potatoes are used. Mix potatoes with a bit of dressing. Season with salt and pepper. Sprinkle with chives.

Combine ham, chicken, sausage, celery strips and red pepper strips in a bowl. Add part of dressing and coat well.

Arrange lettuce on large platter. Place meat mixture in center. Place tuna chunks at one end. Place potatoes at other end. Arrange sardines next to potato. Place egg halves in another area and overlap with anchovy strips. Place tomato quarters next to egg. Arrange onion and pepper rings over tomatoes and potatoes. Decorate with olives and radishes. (If you like another way of arranging this composition, by all means do so). Drizzle entire salad with remaining dressing. Sprinkle with chopped fresh herbs. Serve chilled.

*To julienne, cut in narrow strips.

SALADE NICOISE DRESSING

1 Large egg
½ Cup plus 1 tablespoon light olive oil
3 Tablespoons vinegar (4% acidity) or lemon juice

½ Teaspoon salt, or more, to taste
15 Grindings black pepper
2 Tablespoons whipping cream
1 Tablespoon drained capers

In blender or mixer blend egg, oil, vinegar, salt and pepper, and whipping cream. Add capers and mix. Adjust vinegar to suit your individual taste.

TABBOULEH SALAD
Serves 6-8

2 Cups Bulgar wheat
4 Cups boiling water
½ Cup minced onion
¾ Cup minced parsley
¼ Cup chopped spearmint
1 Cup minced celery
⅓ Cup olive oil

¼ Cup lemon juice
2 Cups tomatoes, peeled,
   seeded and chopped
Salt and freshly
   ground pepper
Salad greens

Place bulgar in a bowl and pour over it the boiling water. Allow to stand until lukewarm or until wheat is expanded and fluffy. Drain off excess water, and shake in colander or sieve until dry. Add onion, parsley, mint, celery, oil, lemon juice, salt and pepper. Chill several hours or overnight. Just before serving add tomatoes. Mound on salad greens.

THE TOSSED GREEN SALAD

The universal favorite. But an awful bore with the same old lettuce and onion and the same old dressing. There is an endless array of possibilities to indulge your pleasure as an Artist at the Salad Bowl. The following merely scratch the surface. Mix and match.

GREENS	VEGETABLES	HERBS	CONDIMENTS, ETC
Lettuce, all kinds	Sliced mushrooms	Chives	Olives
Spinach	Sliced radishes	Parsley	Water chestnuts
Swiss Chard	Sliced cucumbers	Tarragon	Jerusalem artichokes
Mustard Greens	Sliced zucchini	Dill	Garbanzo beans
Dandelion Greens	Diced avocado	Fennel	Pickled beets
Sorrel	Artichoke hearts	Marjoram	Sunflower seeds
Nasturtium leaves	Sliced onion rings	Oregano	Sesame seeds
Escarole	Chopped green pepper	Rosemary	Croutons
Chicory	Minced green onions	Savory	Bacon bits
Beet tops	Cherry tomatoes	Garlic	Toasted filberts
Watercress	Quartered tomatoes	Basil	Walnuts or almonds
Mung bean sprouts	**FRUITS**	Cilantro	Hard-cooked eggs
Alfalfa sprouts	Orange, grapefruit or		Cubed cheeses
Other sprouts	mandarin orange segments		Grated cheeses
	Diced apples		Capers

41

After you have selected your greens, handle tenderly, in order not to bruise. Separate leaves and wash quickly in running water. Allow to drain in colander or lettuce basket. Place leaves on one of your discarded turkish towels, roll up carefully and place in refrigerator to crisp. If overnight, all the better.

When ready to assemble salad, sprinkle salad bowl with salt and rub with a cut clove of garlic. Tear leaves into bite-size pieces. Add other ingredients and wait for the moment of serving to toss with the dressing. Add sunflower, sesame or other seeds after salad has been tossed with dressing.

The classic French way of adding dressing is as follows: Combine greens and seasonings, then gently mix in the oil, and finally the vinegar, tasting as you go. Try it sometime.

VEGETABLE COMBINATION SALAD

A favorite salad in our family was my mother's cooked vegetable salad. She made it in such huge quantities for family gatherings that the kids nicknamed it "Elephant Salad". Content varied according to season. Cook vegetables separately. A good place for leftovers.

Cooked, diced potatoes	Thinly sliced celery
Cooked string beans, cut in	Chopped green onion
½-inch sections	*Diced cucumber
Cooked, diced carrots,	Shredded lettuce
or whole, if tiny	Fresh chopped dill and
Cooked peas	parsley
Thinly sliced radishes	Basic French Dressing
	(Page 43)

Chill all ingredients except dressing. Toss with dressing. Arrange in a bowl lined with salad greens. Garnish with ripe olives, tomato wedges, green and/or red pepper rings, sliced or quartered hard-boiled eggs, etc.

*Peel, dice, salt and allow to stand at least 2 hours, then drain before adding to salad.

DRESSINGS

DIETERS' HERB DRESSING   ¾ Cup

Good with cooked or raw vegetables and tossed greens. Adds zest to plain mayonnaise. Place ingredients in a jar and shake well. Refrigerate.

½ Cup lemon juice or
  wine vinegar
1 Teaspoon dry mustard or
  2 teaspoons Dijon or
  domestic prepared mustard
3 Tablespoons water

1 Teaspoon capers
1 Teaspoon each minced
  parsley, chives
  and marjoram
¼ Teaspoon salt, or to taste
  A few grindings
  black pepper.

DIETERS' BUTTERMILK DRESSING   ⅔ Cup

This zestful dressing is particularly good on tossed greens, citrus fruit salads or cole slaw.

½ Cup buttermilk or yogurt
4 Teaspoons horseradish
1 Teaspoon sugar

1/8 Teaspoon dry mustard
1/8 Teaspoon salt
  A few grindings
  black pepper

Place ingredients in a covered jar and shake. Refrigerate. Shake well before serving.

BASIC FRENCH DRESSING   2 Cups

Also known as "oil and vinegar" and "vinaigrette".

1½ Cups olive oil or other
  good-quality vegetable oil
½ Cup wine vinegar

1 Teaspoon salt, or to taste
  A few grindings
  black pepper

Blend all ingredients. You may wish to adjust the vinegar content to suit your taste and the salad ingredients you are using. Vinegars do vary in acidity.

Apple cider vinegar, rice vinegar or lemon juice may be substituted for wine vinegar.

VARIATIONS

The following are good with green salads, sliced tomatoes and/or raw or cooked vegetables.

VARIATION #1

1 Recipe Basic French
  Dressing
1 Clove garlic, crushed and
  removed before serving

½ Teaspoon *each* dry mustard,
  sugar and paprika
1 Teaspoon Worcestershire
  sauce

VARIATION #2

Columbia River Kitchen's House Dressing, from Carol Madison.

1 Recipe Basic French
  Dressing
2 Teaspoons Worcestershire sauce
½ Cup sugar

¼ Cup grated onion
⅔ Cup catsup

VARIATION #3 — HERB DRESSING

1 Recipe Basic French Dressing
1 Teaspoon *each* fresh thyme leaves, parsley, oregano, tarragon
  and basil, minced; or ½ teaspoon of each, dried

You may decide to use just tarragon, which is a wonderful salad herb. Or just basil, wonderful on tomatoes. Dill is perfect with cucumbers. Rosemary and oregano go well with green salads with citrus fruit segments added; or to give salads an Italian accent.

All the above are merely suggestions. You may, for instance, prefer Dijon mustard to the dry mustard in Variation #1. Nothing is written in concrete.

MAYONNAISE BASE DRESSINGS

*Noticed the price tag on mayonnaise lately? Even **imitation** mayonnaise (Heaven forbid!)? Try making your own, and when you discover how fast and easy it is to make, how much better it tastes, and how much **cheaper** it is, you'll never buy it again if you can help it. And then, you know exactly what's in it.*

BLENDER MAYONNAISE   1¼ Cups

1 Large egg
½ Teaspoon dry mustard
¼ Teaspoon salt
¼ Teaspoon pepper

2 Tablespoons vinegar
1 Cup olive oil or other
    good quality vegetable oil

Place into container of blender the egg, dry ingredients, vinegar and ¼ of the oil. Cover container and turn on lowest speed. Immediately uncover and start pouring in steadily the remainder of the oil, taking no longer than a total of 15 seconds from the time of turning on the motor. Turn on high speed and blend 10 seconds longer.

Taste for seasoning. Transfer to covered container. Refrigerate.

MUSTARD MAYONNAISE

Good with cold meats. Mix 1 cup mayonnaise with 2 tablespoons or more Dijon or domestic prepared mustard.

BLEU CHEESE DRESSING   2 Cups

One of the all-time favorites for green and vegetable salads.

1 Cup mayonnaise
½ Cup bleu cheese,
  finely crumbled

½ Cup buttermilk
1 Clove garlic

Place all ingredients in blender and blend at high speed for 10 seconds. If you are mixing by hand, squeeze juice from garlic and discard remainder, or mince extremely fine.

THOUSAND ISLAND DRESSING   1½ Cups

Excellent for greens, vegetable and seafood salads.

1 Cup mayonnaise
2 Tablespoons catsup
¼ Cup chili sauce
2 Tablespoons minced parsley

1 Tablespoon minced green
  onion tops or chives
Salt and pepper to taste

Blend all ingredients thoroughly. Chill.

GREEN GODDESS DRESSING   1¾ Cups

Excellent with greens, vegetables and fish.

1 Cup mayonnaise
½ Cup sour cream
⅓ Cup minced parsley
3 Tablespoons minced chives
  or green onion tops

1 Tablespoon anchovy paste
  or 2 tablespoons mashed
  anchovy fillets
2 Teaspoons fresh tarragon
  or 1 teaspoon, dried
1 Tablespoon vinegar

Blend all ingredients thoroughly. Chill at least 2 hours.

REMOULADE DRESSING

2 Cups

Excellent with seafood.

1 Recipe Green Goddess
  Dressing, but omit
  sour cream
2 Tablespoons Dijon mustard
1 Tablespoon minced gherkins

1 Tablespoon chopped capers
1 Garlic clove, minced
1 Hard-cooked egg,
  finely chopped
  Dash hot pepper sauce

Combine ingredients well. Chill.

The John Gellatly mansion, corner Okanogan and Kittitas, Wenatchee. Later a nurses' home, then the site of Deaconess Hospital, since abandoned.

Rosilyn Robbins

MAIN DISHES

BEEF & VEAL DISHES & SAUCES

There are those who say beef is on its way out—that seafood is the wave of the future. Others aver it's poultry; still others, grains and vegetables. Who knows? Meanwhile, beef still occupies an impressive percentage of the meat counter, so until it becomes as obsolete as Calves' Foot Soup with Poached Eggs, here are a few favorites to commemorate the days when it reigned supreme.

PORK DISHES & SAUCES

POULTRY DISHES AND SAUCES

Yes, we've gone overboard on chicken, but when you consider value for your nutrition dollar, you can't beat it. A comparatively new item in the markets is ground turkey, so substitute for ground beef or chicken when convenient.

MAIN DISHES

LAMB DISHES

FISH & SEAFOOD

EGG DISHES AND SAUCES

PASTA DISHES AND SAUCES

GAME DISHES AND ACCOMPANIMENTS

Columbia River Country is game country. A few of these recipes are reprinted from out-of-print Columbia River Cook Books. Others are just for fun.

BEEF & VEAL DISHES & SAUCES

BELGIAN BEEF STEW
Serves 8

Columbia River Kitchen catered a big pot of stew for 50 citizens for Riverfront Development on the rolling riverfront lawn owned at that time by Rich Congdon and the John Jacobsons.

There are endless variations on the stew theme. Substitute a cup of Burgundy wine for the beer, add perhaps a teaspoon of rosemary and your dish could be French Provencal. Substitute tomatoes for Beef Stock, a cup or two of dry red or white wine for the beer, add a teaspoon of dried basil and your stew has an accent Italiano. Whatever the style, a green salad, crusty French bread and a glass of Zinfandel or Cabernet Sauvignon make it an Occasion.

½ **Cup all-purpose flour**
1 **Teaspoon salt**
  Few grindings black pepper
1 **Teaspoon celery salt**
½ **Teaspoon thyme leaves**
4 **Pounds beef chuck, cut in 1-inch to 1½-inch cubes**
¼ **Cup vegetable oil (olive oil for French and Italian versions)**
¼ **Cup (½ cube) butter**
2 **Cups chopped onions**
5 **Garlic cloves, minced**

3 **Cups well-seasoned Beef Stock (Page 23) or**
2 **10½-ounce cans beef beef bouillon**
2 **12-ounce cans beer**
2 **Tablespoons brown sugar**
2 **Bay leaves**
¼ **Cup minced parsley**
8 **Small carrots, scraped and cut into 1-inch chunks**
8-10 **Small new potatoes, scrubbed; or 3 cups potatoes cut in 1-inch cubes**
2 **Tablespoons apple cider vinegar**

Mix flour, salt, pepper, celery salt and thyme in a paper bag. Dump in the meat and shake to coat evenly. Heat half of oil and butter in heavy skillet. Over medium-high heat brown meat on all sides. Add remaining oil and butter as needed. Remove meat from pan with a slotted spoon and set aside. In same pan cook onions and garlic until onions are transparent and golden brown. Add beef stock or bouillon, beer, brown sugar and bay leaves. Bring to boiling, stirring to incorporate browned juices. Turn meat and contents of skillet into large stew pot. Bring to boiling, reduce heat, cover tightly and simmer 2 hours. Add carrots, potatoes and parsley and simmer 30 to 45 minutes longer, until vegetables are tender when pierced. Remove from heat. Skim excess fat. Add vinegar and serve.

OLD-FASHIONED BOILED DINNER   Serves 4

This inexpensive meal in a pot has been a family favorite for 60 years. Ham and various inexpensive cuts of beef may be used, the bones adding richness to the broth. A comforting dish, especially inviting at the end of a cold winter day.

4 Pounds lean beef shortribs	8 Small onions, peeled
1 Bay leaf	8 Medium carrots, scraped
¼ Teaspoon peppercorns	1 Medium head cabbage,
1½ Teaspoons salt	cut in wedges
	4 Medium potatoes, peeled

Place shortribs in large kettle with water to barely cover. Add bay leaf, peppercorns and salt. Bring to boiling, reduce heat and simmer 2 hours, covered. Remove from heat. Remove meat and bay leaf. Skim excess fat and strain. Remove bones and excess fat from meat. Return broth to kettle. Add onions and carrots. Layer with the meat. Top with cabbage. Wedge potatoes in vacant spaces. Cover closely, bring to boiling, reduce heat and simmer until vegetables are tender—45 minutes to an hour. Correct seasoning.

To serve, arrange meat and vegetables on heated platter. Pour pot liquor in a bowl to serve as an accompaniment. Have mustard and horseradish on the table for the meat, and wine vinegar to sprinkle on the cabbage, if desired.

VARIATION

CORNED BEEF AND CABBAGE: Substitute corned beef for the shortribs.

OLD-FASHIONED POT ROAST   Serves 6

A tried-and-true Sunday dinner served dozens of times over the years in our family. With the price of beef skyrocketing and becoming less "fashionable," perhaps it's "thanks for the memory".

1 7-Bone Prime beef roast,	1 Dozen small onions, peeled
1½-inches thick	2 Cups cleaned,
8 Tablespoons (½ cup)	sliced mushrooms
all-purpose flour, divided	6 Medium carrots, scraped
3 Tablespoons Worcestershire	(more, if desired)
sauce	6 Medium potatoes, peeled
1 Teaspoon salt	
Few grindings black pepper	

Preheat oven to 325 degrees F. Cut edge of roast in 2 or 3 places to prevent curling. Rub 2 tablespoons flour on each side of roast and brown each side under broiler. Place in roasting pan and sprinkle with Worcestershire sauce, salt and pepper. Place onions on top of roast, carrots around the edge where they will be in contact with the juices. Arrange mushrooms over the onions. Bake, covered, about 3 to 3½ hours, or until meat is tender. Add potatoes during the last 2 hours of cooking At this time rearrange the vegetables, placing the carrots on top of the roast, and the potatoes around the edge where they can absorb juices and turn a nice golden brown. When roast is tender, remove roast and vegetables from baking pan, arrange on heated platter and keep warm.

To make gravy, skim off fat and add enough water to pan juices to measure 3 cups. Measure ¼ cup cold water in a bowl. Blend in 4 table-spoons flour until no lumps remain. Bring pan juices to boiling and add flour mixture, stirring constantly while adding, until thickened. Simmer 3 minutes. Remove from heat. Correct seasoning.

Mashed potatoes are delicious with pot roast, as well as noodles.

ROAST MARINATED TENDERLOIN OF BEEF
Serves 6

For the visiting VIP. Serve with STUFFED MUSHROOMS (Page 123), GREEN BEANS JULIENNE (Page 122), CRÊPES AU FROMAGE (Page 152) *and* STRAWBERRIES ROMANOFF (Page 162).

1 4-pound tenderloin of beef

MARINADE
½ Cup *each* red wine, Worcestershire sauce and olive oil
3 Garlic cloves, chopped

1 Teaspoon peppercorns
½ Teaspoon salt
1 Bay leaf
1 Teaspoon thyme leaves

Tie the beef with string at intervals to form a compact cylinder. Mix marinade ingredients. Place beef in plastic bag, pour in the marinade and close bag securely. Place in a dish in the refrigerator and marinate for 24 hours or more, turning the bag frequently.

Preheat oven to 425 degrees F. Remove beef from bag and scrape off any bits of the marinade that cling. Place meat in roasting pan in the center of the oven for about 45 minutes, or until meat thermometer registers 140. Remove meat and lower setting to 350 for the stuffed mushrooms, if desired. Allow roast to rest 15 minutes. Carve, catching juices for the platter.

STEAK DIANE   Serves 2

Years ago I peeked into the kitchen of Wenatchee's Cottage Inn and was fascinated by the sight of old-fashioned flatirons sitting atop the steaks sizzling on the range. This practice undoubtedly had something to do with their wonderful juicy tenderness. I don't use flatirons, but have learned over the years that pounding certain boneless steaks prior to pan broiling improves them tremendously.

Potatoes Dauphinoise, fresh steamed asparagus, green beans julienne or broccoli, a good California Cabernet Sauvignon and candlelight should accompany Steak Diane. Have the table set, the ingredients assembled and ready to go, since this is a fast, last-minute, stove-to-table operation.

2 **Tenderloin steaks, 6 to 8-ounces each**	1 **Tablespoons Worcestershire sauce**
4 **Tablespoons butter, softened**	2 **Teaspoons Dijon mustard**
2 **Teaspoons finely chopped chives or green onion tops**	¼ **Cup dry white or red wine** **Few grindings black pepper**
2 **Tablespoons cognac or brandy**	

Trim fat from meat and snip membrane to prevent curling. Place steaks between sheets of wax paper and pound to ¼-inch to 3/8-inch thickness. (I use my iron frying pan). Blend chives with 2 tablespoons of the butter. Set aside. In 10-inch skillet heat remaining butter over high heat until just begining to brown, but not smoking. Add the steaks and cook about 2 minutes on each side for medium rare. Meanwhile heat cognac or brandy in a small pan. Remove from heat. Ignite and pour flaming over the steaks. Remove steaks to heated plates and keep hot. Add Worcestershire sauce, mustard, wine and pepper to pan juices. Heat and stir until bubbling. Spread chive butter over steaks and spoon pan juices over. Serve immediately.

When Prince Charles visited, Nancy Reagan fed him cold loin of beef with horseradish, Long Island duckling with bing cherry sauce and cold lobster with mustard mayonnaise, topped off with California strawberries in heavy New Jersey cream. He said that he ate too much.

VARIATIONS

Lean ground beef patties (hamburgers) and less expensive cuts of beef such as minute steaks, boneless chuck or round steaks become gourmet specialties when glamorized à la Diane. Domestic prepared mustard may be substituted for Dijon mustard.

BETTY'S SIRLOIN STEAK
Serves 4

This recipe was the rage around town for a couple of years during the '50s, given to me by Betty Skillern. The butcher needs a bit of notice.

1 Center cut sirloin steak, 2-inches thick, round bone at the side
¼ Teaspoon garlic salt
1 Small onion, minced

1 Small green pepper, chopped
¾ Cup catsup
1 Teaspoon Worcestershire sauce

Preheat oven to 400 degrees F. Place steak on shallow baking pan. Mix all remaining ingredients and pour over steak. Bake 25 minutes.

CHINESE PEPPER STEAK
Serves 2-3

Chinese Pepper Steak was popular with Columbia River Kitchen customers. Fast and easy.

1 Pound flank steak
1 Tablespoon cornstarch
1 Teaspoon sugar
3 Tablespoons soy sauce, or to taste
1 Tablespoon dry white wine

2 Large green peppers, cut into 1-inch squares
4 Tablespoons vegetable oil, divided
¼ Teaspoon salt
1 Clove garlic, minced

Cut steak across the grain into paper-thin slices, slanting the knife almost horizontally with cutting board. In a bowl, combine cornstarch, sugar, soy sauce and wine, and mix with the sliced steak. Pour 2 tablespoons of the oil into skillet over high heat. Add salt and green peppers. Stir constantly until peppers turn darker green—about 2 minutes. Remove peppers with slotted spoon. Add remaining oil to skillet with minced garlic. Stir in the beef mixture. Cook, stirring constantly, for about 2 minutes. Add green peppers. Mix well.

Serve immediately with PLAIN STEAMED RICE (Page 131).

LONDON BROIL

Serves 3 or 4

1 Flank steak,
1 Recipe Marinade
(Page 7)

Béarnaise Sauce

Follow preparation procedure given for London Broil in Appetizer Section. Serve with Béarnaise Sauce.

BÉARNAISE SAUCE

1 Recipe Hollandaise
(Page 88)
¼ Cup dry white wine
2 Tablespoons lemon juice
1 Tablespoon minced shallots
or onion

1 Tablespoon minced fresh
tarragon or 2 teaspoons,
dried
Few grindings black pepper

Make Hollandaise and leave in blender container. In small saucepan combine wine, lemon juice, shallots or onion, tarragon and pepper. Bring to boiling and cook rapidly until liquid is reduced to about 2 tablespoons or less. Cool slightly. Add to Hollandaise. Blend at high speed for 10 seconds. Correct seasoning. Add more tarragon if desired.

CORNED BEEF HASH

Serves 6

An old-timer—super for breakfast, brunch or supper. Top with a poached egg, if desired.

3 Tablespoons butter
½ Cup minced onion
3 Cups cooked, chopped
corned beef
3 Cups cooked, finely
diced potatoes

½ Cup minced parsley
¼ Cup minced celery
½ Cup light cream
Salt and freshly ground
pepper to taste

In a skillet over medium heat cook onion in butter until transparent. In a medium bowl mix all remaining ingredients. Add the onion. The amount of cream may vary according to moisture content of other ingredients. Add just enough to hold together. Form into cakes. Add a little more butter to skillet if it seems too dry, heat and cook cakes on both sides until nicely browned.

"The discovery of a new dish does more for the happiness of man than the discovery of a new star."

Serves 4

SWEDISH KAALDOLMER (Stuffed Cabbage Leaves)

An all-time family favorite, a popular specialty at Columbia River Kitchen. Perfect for a party. Serve with mashed or boiled potatoes.

1 Medium head cabbage
2 Tablespoons raw rice,
  or 4 tablespoons cooked
½ Cup chopped onion
2 Tablespoons butter
½ Pound lean ground beef
  or ground veal
½ Pound lean ground pork
1 Large egg
1 Teaspoon salt
Few grindings black pepper

2 Bay leaves
1 Teaspoon ground sage or
  2 teaspoons, fresh
3 Medium fresh, ripe
  tomatoes, or
  1½ cups canned
3 Tablespoons all-purpose
  flour
1 Cup light cream

Cut out center core of cabbage and place core side down in a pot of boiling water to cover. Remove from heat and let stand, covered, for 10 minutes. Boil rice for 15 minutes in 2 cups of water (if you do not have leftover cooked rice). Drain. In a small frying pan over medium-high heat cook onion in butter until transparent. Remove cabbage from water and drain, core side down.

In a medium bowl mix beef, pork, cooked onion, egg, salt and pepper. Separate cabbage leaves carefully. Place a cylinder of meat mixture on the leafy end and roll up. This will vary according to size of leaves. If leaves are small, a rounded tablespoon may be enough. If leaves are large, as much as ¼ cup. Roll once to cover meat and overlap both sides to completely enclose cylinder before completing the rolling process. Fasten with a toothpick if you feel it is necessary. At this point brown the rolls on both sides in butter. This is optional.

Place rolls in 6-quart saucepan or dutch oven. Add bay leaves, sage, tomatoes and enough boiling water to almost cover. Taste for seasoning. Cover, bring to boiling, reduce heat and simmer one hour. Remove bay leaves.

Blend flour and cream until smooth. Remove rolls from pot with slotted spoon and place in large serving dish. Bring liquid in pot to boiling, add flour and cream mixture gradually, stirring until thickened. Simmer 3 minutes. Taste for seasoning. Pour over cabbage rolls.

VARIATION

STUFFED PEPPERS: To serve 6, seed and core 6 large green peppers. Place in large saucepan, cover with water and parboil 5 minutes. Drain completely. Include and follow directions for combining ingredients beginning with rice through salt and pepper. Stuff peppers. Sprinkle with breadcrumbs and dot with butter. Place in buttered baking dish. Add ¼ cup water. Cover and bake 45 minutes in 350 degree F. oven.

PIROSHKI   Serves 8

Try a Russian dinner with openers of thinly sliced hard sausage such as summer sausage, pickles and radishes, BORSTCH *(Page 25);* PIROSHKI *and* FRESH PLUM *or* APRICOT PUDDING *(Page 158). The pastry, incidentally, makes a loaf of delicious bread.*

PASTRY

1 Cup *hot* tap water	1 Large egg
3 Tablespoons butter or vegetable oil	1 Tablespoon (1 envelope) dry yeast
1 Teaspoon salt	3½ Cups unbleached
1 Tablespoon honey	all-purpose flour

Place in a small bowl the hot water, butter or oil, salt, honey, egg and yeast, in that order. Allow to stand until yeast bubbles up and foams, about 15 minutes, depending on temperature of the room. Measure flour into bowl and make a well in the center. Pour in the yeast mixture and stir together until well blended and formed into a ball. If too soft and sticky add more flour. Turn out on lightly floured board and knead until smooth and springy, about 5 minutes. Place dough in lightly oiled bowl. Cover with a towel and allow to rise until doubled. When ready a hole will remain if you poke your finger into the dough. While dough is rising make the filling. This filling may also be made in advance and refrigerated or frozen.

FILLING

1 Tablespoon butter	1 Cup sauerkraut, washed,
1 Cup finely chopped onion	squeezed dry and packed
½ Pound lean ground beef	⅓ Cup dry bread crumbs
½ Pound lean ground pork	1½ Cups sour cream,
½ Teaspoon salt or to taste	part for garnish
Few grindings black pepper	1 Egg, fork beaten with 1
1 Teaspoon dill weed; fresh,	tablespoon water, for glaze
if available	1 Tablespoon poppy seeds

Melt butter in large frying pan over medium-high heat. Cook onion and meat, stirring frequently, until onion is transparent and meat is browned. Drain excess fat. Add seasonings, sauerkraut, crumbs and ½ cup of the sour cream. Mix well and correct seasoning.

Divide pastry and roll out one-half at a time on lightly floured surface to 1/8-inch thickness. Cut into 6-inch squares. Place ½ cup filling in center of square. Elongate filling into sausage shape. Fold one edge of pastry over filling. Moisten top rim of dough with water and fold over other edge. Press lightly to seal. Moisten bottom inside rim of each end. Bring up over ends to seal. Turn Piroshki over so that sealed edge is on the bottom. Turn ends under securely so that a neat "pillow" results. Place Piroshkis on lightly oiled baking sheet. Allow to rise 30 minutes. Brush lightly with glaze. Sprinkle with poppy seeds. Bake in 350 degree F. oven for 30 to 35 minutes, until golden brown. Serve hot. Garnish with sour cream.

See COCKTAIL PIROSHKI: (Page 4).

PORK DISHES & SAUCES

BAKED BEANS
Serves 8

Beans have a problem that is revealed in a popular chant of my grade school days: "Silence in the courtroom—the judge is eating beans!" This protein-rich legume, so universally eaten and enjoyed, does not deserve such a blot on its escutcheon. And we do have it in our power to remedy the problem. Soda is the answer.

Saturday night and Baked Beans are a New England tradition. Serve with CORNBREAD (Page 147), *a green salad and apple pie.*

4 Cups Great Northern or
   navy beans
½ Teaspoon baking soda
   (optional)
2 Teaspoons salt
1 Teaspoon dry mustard
¼ Cup molasses or
   brown sugar

1 Medium onion, chopped
1 Clove garlic, minced
1 Pound lean slab bacon,
   cut in 1-inch chunks
½ Cup catsup (optional)

Pick over and wash beans. Cover with at least 4 inches of water and soak overnight. Next day, if you are using soda, add to the soaked beans and bring to boiling. Reduce heat and simmer, covered, for 30 minutes. Drain. Add fresh boiling water and simmer until just tender when pierced.

If you are not using soda, drain the soaked beans, add fresh cold water and bring to boiling. Reduce heat and simmer, covered, for an hour or until beans are just tender when pierced. Do not overcook to mushiness.

Preheat oven to 250 degrees F. Place half the beans and bean water in a bean pot or casserole. Add the salt, mustard, molasses or brown sugar, onion, garlic, the cut-up bacon and remaining beans. If there is not enough water to just barely cover the beans, add boiling water. Pour catsup over the top if desired.

Cover and bake 6 or 7 hours, adding boiling water if beans start to dry out. Remove lid during the last hour of baking. Do not add water, but permit·the top to turn a nice crusty brown.

CANNED BAKED BEANS WITH FRANKFURTERS

*If you haven't time to go through the above process and you yearn for beans, try the following. When you open the can you'll find not an abundance of lean, succulent chunks of cooked bacon, but one yucky hunk of disintegrating fat. This is definitely **not** a gourmet creation, but lots of people like it.*

Open a #2½ can of baked beans. Spread in casserole or baking dish. Layer with frankfurters. Plop catsup over all. Bake in 350 oven until heated through and the frankfurters are lightly browned.

HERITAGE HAM LOAF
Serves 6

Recycled is Reborn! The remnants of a Christmas ham found a final resting place in this delicious loaf and vanished without a trace in sandwiches, sliced cold.

1 Pound pork sausage
2 Cups finely ground
    smoked ham
3 Eggs
1 Cup dry bread or
    cracker crumbs

1 Cup light cream
½ Cup catsup
    Salt and freshly
    ground pepper

Preheat oven to 350 degrees F. Combine all ingredients. Form a loaf. Place in buttered baking pan and pour over the Ham Sauce. Bake 1½ hours. Baste 3 or 4 times.

HAM SAUCE

¼ Cup vinegar
½ Cup pineapple juice
¼ Cup water
½ Cup brown sugar

1 Tablespoon dry mustard
½ Teaspoon ground ginger
Few dashes Worcestershire
sauce

Combine all ingredients in saucepan. Boil for one minute.

See HAM POOPOOS in Appetizer Section.

SAUERKRAUT AND SPARERIBS   Serves 6

Sauerkraut and spareribs and sauerkraut with our own sausage were dishes we often enjoyed on the farm in Hobart. You will find variations of this recipe in gourmet magazines under the name "Choucroute," a famous dish of Alsace.

I tasted Choucroute in Ribeauvillé, a picturesque Alsatian village. Piled on the sauerkraut were a frankfurter, sliced ham, smoked bacon and sausage, with small whole boiled potatoes on the side. Dessert was an interesting and delicious combination of mocha ice cream, cooked dried prunes and Eau de Vie. In Frankfurt a restaurant called Dippegucker served sauerkraut and spareribs that tasted exactly like my mother's.

Serve with pumpernickel or rye bread, or coarse French bread. And beer or Johannisberg Riesling.

1½ Quarts sauerkraut
4 Pounds pork spareribs,
  cut in serving pieces
2 Tablespoons chicken fat
  or butter
2 Cups chopped onions
1 Teaspoon caraway seeds
6 Small, whole potatoes with
  skins, scrubbed clean

Salt and freshly
ground pepper
2 Tablespoons honey
1 Cup Chicken Stock
(Page 16), or
equivalent, canned

Place sauerkraut in colander and rinse with cold water to remove excess sharpness. You will find that this precaution will give you an entirely new and inspired outlook on sauerkraut. Broil spareribs on both sides until golden brown. Drain fat, but reserve drippings, if any and add to sauerkraut later. In frying pan heat chicken fat or butter. Add onions and cook until transparent. Mix sauerkraut, onions and caraway seeds. Preheat oven to 350 degrees F.

Place half of sauerkraut mixture in ovenproof casserole. Add drippings, if any. Layer with potatoes. Sprinkle with salt and pepper. Spread with remaining sauerkraut. Drizzle with honey. Pour in chicken stock. Top with spareribs. Salt and pepper. Bake covered for 1½ hours, or until spareribs and potatoes are tender. Check from time to time, and add more chicken stock if necessary to prevent drying out. (When finished there should be very little or no liquid remaining.)

Remove from oven. Taste for seasoning. Place sauerkraut on platter, spareribs over the top and potatoes around the edge.

VARIATION

CHOUCROUTE: Substitute for the spareribs one or more of the following: Polish sausage, knockwurst, plain or smoked pork chops, bacon chunks, pig's knuckles, ham, chicken or goose. Substitute dry white wine for the chicken stock. Add garlic and/or bay leaf if you like. Another idea is to substitute a dozen juniper berries and ⅓ cup gin for the caraway seeds and chicken stock. The sky's the limit.

See also BARBECUED HONOLULU PORK SPARERIBS, KEBABS (Page 66).

GLEANED FROM CHELAN COUNTY REPUBLICAN WOMEN'S CLUB BULLETIN:

"Propoganda is baloney disguised as food for thought".

POULTRY DISHES & SAUCES

HAWAIIAN CUISINE

Hawaii is a gastronomic Paradise reflecting the rich, cosmopolitan mingling of Polynesian, Oriental and "haole" cookery. This melting pot of Hawaiians, Samoans, Chinese, Japanese, Koreans, Filipinos, Puerto Ricans, Americans, British, Portuguese, Germans, French and others has produced a fascinating cuisine.

When I lived in Honolulu during the thirties the only Waikiki hotels were the Royal Hawaiian and Moana, now almost totally obscured by the sea of high rise. But nothing has changed the wonderful fruits and vegetables, the fish so fresh you can eat them raw, and the endless ethnic food varieties.

CHICKEN HEKKA (Japanese) Serves 6

Chicken Sukiyaki is one of the all-time Hawaiian favorites. You will find in Hawaiian markets packages of chicken marked "Cut for Hekka". This is fine if you don't mind coping with a welter of cut-up bones along with the meat. I personally prefer the boneless route. Serve this dish with plain boiled or steamed rice, hot sake in tiny cups, and Japanese tea.

2-3 Pounds chicken breasts and thighs, boned
6 Green onions
1½ Cups celery, thinly sliced diagonally
½ Cup green beans, sliced julienne; or Chinese pea pods
1 Cup thinly sliced onions
1 Clove garlic, minced
½ Teaspoon grated fresh ginger

2 Cups canned bamboo shoots
2 Cups sliced fresh mushrooms
3 Tablespoons peanut oil
½ Cup sake or dry white wine
3 Tablespoons sugar
½ Cup soy sauce
Chinese parsley (Cilantro) for garnish

Organize ingredients. Slice chicken into ¼-inch pieces across the grain. Prepare vegetables. In one bowl place the white part of the green onions, the celery and green beans or pea pods. In another bowl place the sliced onions, minced garlic, grated ginger, bamboo shoots and mushrooms. Cut the green onion tops into 1-inch lengths and cut into strips lengthwise. Set aside. Wash the Chinese parsley.

Heat large skillet or wok over high heat, add 1 tablespoon of the oil and heat. Add the bowl of vegetables containing green beans, sprinkle with ½ teaspoon of the sugar (to retain color) and cook 2 minutes, stirring. Remove from pan and set aside. Now add another tablespoon of the oil to the skillet or wok, heat and add the bowl of vegetables containing the mushrooms, add ½ teaspoon sugar and cook 3 minutes, stirring. Remove and set aside. Finally, add remaining oil to skillet, heat and add chicken and cook, stirring, 5 minutes. Add sake, remaining sugar and soy sauce. Reduce heat, cover and cook about 5 minutes longer, until chicken is tender. Return all vegetables to pan and fold in gently with the chicken. Taste for seasoning. Add more soy sauce and salt and pepper, if desired. Heat through.

To serve, place rice on platter or individual plates, arrange Hekka on top and garnish with green onion tops and Chinese parsley. Or place the rice in a separate serving bowl. Or serve rice in individual rice bowls. Have a bottle or cruet of soy sauce on the table.

NOTE: Hawaiians use liberal amounts of watercress in their cookery. Good in Chicken Hekka, if obtainable.

HONOLULU CHICKEN   Serves 4

A popular Columbia River Kitchen specialty. Although this recipe specifies broilers, you may of course use cut-up chicken fryers or any parts thereof. Serve with steamed rice or RICE PILAF (Page 130), a green salad and a rich chocolate dessert.

2 Whole broilers (2 pounds each) split in half	¼ Cup minced parsley
3 Tablespoons butter	¼ Cup minced fresh marjoram or Chinese parsley (Cilantro)
3 Tablespoons vegetable oil	½ Cup thinly sliced water chestnuts
½ Cup minced green onion tops or chives	

Preheat oven to 350 degrees F. Rinse broilers and pat dry. Melt half the butter and oil in heavy frying pan over medium-high heat. When bubbling, brown the broilers quickly on both sides, adding remainder of butter and oil as needed. Remove to a 9 x 13 baking dish or casserole large enough to accommodate the chicken in a single layer. Pour over the marinade. Sprinkle with onion, parsley, marjoram and water chestnuts. Cover and seal with foil. Bake one hour, or until chicken is tender.

When ready to serve, remove chicken from baking dish to heated plates. Or serve in the baking dish. Spoon some of the marinade over. Marinade is reusable. Strain and freeze.

TERIYAKI MARINADE (2½ cups)

½ Cup soy sauce
½ Cup sake or dry
   white wine
1½ Cups pineapple juice
1 Tablespoon grated
   fresh ginger

3 Cloves garlic, minced
½ Teaspoon freshly
   ground pepper
1 Teaspoon Accent

Mix all ingredients.

VARIATIONS

BARBECUED HONOLULU CHICKEN: Pour marinade over chicken. Refrigerate 2 to 18 hours. Turn occasionally. Remove from marinade. Broil over charcoal or in oven broiler until tender, basting with marinade.

BARBECUED HONOLULU PORK SPARERIBS: Marinate pork spareribs 2 to 18 hours. Turn occasionally. Remove from marinade. Broil over charcoal or in oven broiler, or bake at 325 degrees until tender, basting occasionally with marinade.

BARBECUED HONOLULU PORK KEBABS: Cut pork shoulder in 1-inch cubes, marinate 4 or 5 hours and broil on skewers with chunks of pepper, a mushroom or two, and chunks of pineapple.

CHICKEN ENCHILADA CRÊPES   16 Crêpes

One of the Columbia River Kitchen favorites. Crêpes, filling, sauce and toppings may all be prepared in advance and refrigerated. Or finish up to the point of baking and freeze. Good with a fresh fruit salad and honey-lemon dressing.

BASIC CRÊPE BATTER

3 Large eggs
1¼ Cups milk
2 Tablespoons melted butter

1 Cup unbleached
   all-purpose flour
1/8 Teaspoon salt

Blend all ingredients until smooth. Let batter rest at room temperature 2 hours or cover and refrigerate overnight.

If you have crêpe maker, prepare according to manufacturer's directions. Otherwise, bake on lightly greased, heated griddle or in heavy frying pan over medium-high heat. Ladle 2 ounces (3 tablespoonfuls) of batter on the griddle and spread to make 6-inch crêpe. Cook about 30 seconds, or until top is covered with bubbles and the under side is a light golden brown. Flip crêpe over and allow to dry for a few seconds. Turn out onto a plate, and continue, overlapping crêpes in a circular pattern to allow for easy detaching when it is time to roll them. Cover with waxed paper to prevent drying.

When ready to roll, place 2 tablespoons filling in the center of the light side, elongating filling towards the edges. Roll up and place in buttered baking dish, seam side down. Pour over Supreme Sauce. Sprinkle with grated cheeses and parsley. Add garnish. Bake uncovered in 350 degree oven until sauce bubbles and crêpes and sauce are golden in color, about 30 minutes.

FILLING

2 Tablespoons butter or vegetable oil
1 Cup chopped onions
¼ Cup chopped green pepper
1 Cup chopped mushrooms
1 Cup chopped celery
1 4-ounce can green chopped chilies
2 Cups diced chicken
¼ Cup minced parsley
1 Teaspoon ground cumin
¾ Cup Supreme Sauce
Salt and pepper to taste

Melt butter in heavy frying pan over high heat. Add onions, green pepper, mushrooms and celery and cook 3 or 4 minutes or until crisp-tender.Remove pan from heat. Add remaining ingredients, blend and add salt and pepper to taste.

SUPREME SAUCE

½ Cup (1 cube) butter, or ½ chicken fat and ½ butter
½ Cup unbleached all-purpose flour
3 Cups boiling Chicken Stock (Page 16) or 2 10¾-ounce cans chicken consomme
½ Cup light cream, or more if needed
Salt and pepper to taste

Melt butter in saucepan, add flour and whisk over medium heat for 3 minutes, or until mixture bubbles well. Add boiling chicken stock all at once, stirring vigorously until thoroughly blended and thickened. Remove from heat, add cream and seasonings. Sauce should be thin enough to pour over the crêpes. Thin with cream or chicken stock, if necessary.

TOPPING

½ Cup minced parsley	½ Cup grated sharp
½ Cup grated Swiss cheese	cheddar cheese

GARNISH
Whole or sliced black olives
Slivered pimientos

VARIATIONS

CHICKEN CHOW MEIN CRÊPES: Substitute 1 cup sliced water chestnuts, Jerusalem artichokes, bamboo shoots or hearts of palm for the chilies. Omit cumin, olives and pimientos. At serving time sprinkle crêpes with Chow Mein noodles.

CHICKEN DIVAN CRÊPES: Eliminate green pepper, chilies and cumin. When rolling crêpes, include one cooked spear of broccoli or asparagus with the filling. Sprinkle topping with paprika. Garnish with black olives, if desired.

CHAMPAGNE CHICKEN   Serves 8

"Miss Crawley had been in France—and loved ever after, French novels, French cookery and French wines".—THACKERAY

Our October tour of the gastronomic centers and wine regions of France brought us the pleasure of a visit with the Moineaux family of Chouilly, a village in Champagne. They produce their own fine champagne from the 6-acre vineyard which has been in their family for generations. This is the basis of their comfortable lifestyle which includes some education of their daughters abroad.

The following is my adaptation of a favorite family recipe Madame Moineaux shared with us. Serve with steamed new potatoes sprinkled with fresh dill, or rice pilaf; steamed broccoli, asparagus or julienned new beans; and a green salad of bibb lettuce. And champagne, of course.

2 Broiler chickens, about 2½ pounds each, cut in quarters; or 5- to 6-pound fryer, cut in serving pieces	½ Lemon Salt and white pepper ½ Cup (1 cube) unsalted butter, divided ¼ Cup cognac or brandy

68

Preheat oven to 325 degrees F. Rub chicken pieces with lemon juice, then salt and pepper. In heavy skillet heat butter until foaming over medium-high heat. Brown chicken pieces on both sides. Place in 9 x 13 baking dish. Bake 30-40 minutes, uncovered, until tender when pierced with a fork. Remove from oven and allow to cool 5 minutes. Heat cognac or brandy, ignite and pour flaming over chicken. Spoon over Champagne Sauce, which you have prepared while chicken has been in the oven. Sprinkle with parsley and serve.

CHAMPAGNE SAUCE

Unsalted butter if needed
½ Cup chopped shallots
  or onions
1 Pound fresh mushrooms,
  cleaned and sliced
2 Cups Chicken Stock
  (Page 15) or equivalent,
  canned

1 Bottle champagne or
  sparkling white wine
  or ½ cup dry
  white Vermouth
1 Cup whipping cream
  Sale and white pepper
  to taste
¼ Cup minced parsley

If needed, add more butter to the frying pan in which chicken was browned, heat and add onions. Cook, stirring, for 2 minutes. Add mushrooms and cook 5 minutes longer. Add chicken stock and champagne or vermouth and boil until reduced by half. Add cream and continue boiling until syrupy. Taste for seasoning. If there are chicken juices in the pan in which chicken has baked, add to sauce and reduce, if necessary.

VARIATION

I have prepared this recipe using boned and skinned breasts and thighs. Chicken breasts cook quickly. Brown in bubbling butter just until tender and a rich golden color, about 4 minutes on each side. Thighs take a little longer. The breasts need not be baked.
*Try Weibel's Green Hungarian sparkling white wine as an alternative.

"The chickens always come home to roost".

Kay Arneil's
CHICKEN WITH WINE
Serves 2

A flavorful dish for calorie watchers.

**2 Whole chicken breasts,
halved; or 2 halves of
chicken breast and 2 thighs
3 Tablespoons vegetable oil**

**1 Cup thinly sliced onions
1 Cup dry white wine
¼ Teaspoon ginger
Salt and white pepper**

Salt and pepper chicken. In heavy frying pan heat oil over medium-high heat, saute chicken pieces until golden brown. Remove from pan. In same pan cook onions, stirring until limp and transparent. Return chicken to pan. Add wine, ginger, salt and pepper. Cover and steam 15 or 20 minutes on low heat, until chicken is tender.

CHICKEN AND DUMPLINGS
Serves 6

Sometimes we poach our chickens. And sometimes we brown the pieces first. Either way, onward to the preservation of a delicious old-fashioned Sunday dinner.

But first, a word about chicken fat. Did you know that early Japanese immigrants to this country ate so little in order to save money to take back to their homeland that eventually they could not see at twilight? Eating the yellow fat of old chickens restored their sight. This reminded me that my stepfather, a Latvian who had served in the Tsarina's Cavalry—"the pick of the tallest and best lookin' men in the Russian Army"—had told us that a common malady in the Russian military was "chicken blindness", as he called it, resulting from poor diet.

Chicken fat was a staple of my mother's cooking. She never threw away the fat, but skimmed it from the broth into jars, to be used later in the preparation of many dishes, such as Chicken and Dumplings.

1 5-7 pound roasting or stewing chicken, cut into serving pieces. If, you wish to brown, dredge in flour and brown in butter. Follow recipe for CHICKEN STOCK (Page 16). Omit carrots, onions and celery in the stock in the beginning. Instead, add during the last hour of cooking, 6 large carrots, scraped and cut in 1-inch chunks, 1½ cups chopped celery and 1½ cups chopped onions.

When chicken and vegetables are tender, remove from stock and set aside. Strain the stock and skim excess fat.

CHICKEN GRAVY

¾ Cup butter or chicken fat
¾ Cup unbleached
all-purpose flour
4 Cups boiling chicken stock

½ Cup minced parsley
Salt and pepper to taste

In 6-quart dutch oven melt butter or chicken fat over medium heat. Add flour, blend and stir until mixture bubbles. Simmer 3 minutes. Add boiling chicken stock all at once, whisking vigorously until thoroughly blended and thickened. Add parsley. Taste for seasoning. Add chicken pieces and vegetables to pot. Bring to boiling, then reduce to lowest heat so gravy will not bubble violently. Be careful not to scorch.

Float 6 heaping tablespoonfuls of dumpling dough 2 to 3 inches apart on top of chicken pieces and vegetables. Be sure not to drop them in the gravy or you'll have soggy dumplings. Cover pot and cook for 15 minutes. *Do not peek.*

DUMPLINGS

1½ Cups *sifted* unbleached
all-purpose flour
½ Teaspoon salt
4 Teaspoons baking powder

⅔ Cup milk
½ Cup minced chives
or parsley

Sift together into a bowl the flour, salt and baking powder. Make a well in the center and pour in the milk, stirring quickly and lightly. Add chives or parsley. The dough should be sticky, heavy and wet, but not too stiff.

CHICKEN AND NOODLES: Follow above recipe. Instead of dumplings, serve with HOMEMADE NOODLES. (Page 25).

CHICKEN OR TURKEY POT PIE   Serves 8

A popular Columbia River Kitchen Wednesday luncheon specialty, and a logical outlet for your leftover chicken or turkey. If you do not have the leftovers and wish to start from scratch, follow instructions for CHICKEN STOCK *(Page 16).*

4 Cups cooked, diced chicken
    or turkey
4 Cups chicken gravy or
    leftover turkey gravy
1 Cup tiny whole
    boiling onions
1½ Cups diced carrots
1½ Cups diced potatoes
½ Cup celery, cut in
    ½-inch pieces
½ Cup water
1 Cup frozen or fresh peas
½ Cup minced parsley

In a medium saucepan place the onions, carrots, potatoes, celery and water. Bring to boiling, reduce heat and steam until just tender. Add parsley. If using fresh peas, add the last five minutes of cooking. If frozen, add with the parsley, cover pan and allow to thaw. If using canned onions, add with the parsley. Bring to simmering and remove from heat. Drain vegetable water into either your chicken gravy, if it needs thinning, or into your vegetable stock bank. (Or drink it). Preheat oven to 375 degrees F.

Divide chicken, vegetables and gravy evenly among 8 earthenware, ovenproof individual pots. Top with BASIC PIE CRUST (Page 181) 1/8-inch thick, cut in circles one inch larger than diameter of pots. Lay circle of dough over top of each pot. Seal by pressing pastry firmly to sides of bowls. If desired, arrange decorative dough cutouts on top, cutting several slits to allow venting of steam. Brush tops with beaten egg. Bake 25 minutes, or until sauce bubbles and crust is a rich golden brown. Serve immediately.

VARIATION

CHICKEN POT PIE WITH BISCUITS: Instead of pastry, serve with BAKING POWDER BISCUITS (Page 146). Divide cooked ingredients and gravy equally among bakeproof pots. Bake until sauce bubbles. Place baked biscuits on top. Serve immediately.

PILAFF DE VOLAILLE A LA GRÈQUE   Serves 6-8

Our October tour of gastronomic and wine centers of France took us to a cooking session at Cordon Bleu in Paris. Since the instruction by Chef Simon was in French the whole thing would have been confusing had it not been for the American students, seemingly delighted to see American tourists, who helped with the translation.

Preliminaries included details such as "Singe the chicken. Cut off feet and remove guts". (I hadn't done that since my growing-up years on the Hobart farm). The chicken used in the demonstration was Poulet de Bresse, grown under strict government specifications and sold with a seal guaranteeing excellence.

We noted with interest that although expensive copper pans decorated the premises and were for sale there, the pans actually used were rather beat-up specimens resembling the ones I use at home.

1 4-5 pound frying chicken, cut in serving pieces	2 Tablespoons flour
Salt and pepper	2 Cups Chicken (Page 16) or Beef Stock (Page 23)
Flour for dredging chicken	1 Bouquet garni (1 celery
2 Tablespoons unsalted butter, or more if needed	stalk, 6-inch piece of green onion or leek, 1 bay leaf,
1 Large onion, minced	4 parsley stems, 1 thyme
1 Large red pepper, chopped in 1-inch pieces	stalk, tied with string). Salt and pepper to taste
1 Large green pepper, chopped in 1-inch pieces	½ Cup raisins puffed in ½ cup boiling water

Pour boiling water over raisins. Let stand. Prepare 2 bouquet garni: one for the chicken and one for the Pilaff. (If you do not have thyme stalks, add a pinch of dried thyme leaves to chicken and to Pilaff.)

You will need 2 large skillets or dutch ovens, since you will be cooking the chicken and Pilaff at the same time.

Prepare chicken pieces. Bone breasts and cut each half in 3 pieces across the grain. Salt and pepper chicken and dredge in flour. Melt butter in heavy frying pan over medium-high heat. Brown chicken on both sides. Remove from pan and set aside. Preheat oven to 375 degrees F. Add onion to frying pan. Saute 2 minutes. Add green and red pepper. Cook 5 minutes, stirring. Return chicken to skillet. Mix with the vegetables. Sprinkle with flour and mix thoroughly. Add chicken or beef stock. Add bouquet garni, salt and pepper and the raisins and water. Bring to boiling, cover and bake for 20 minutes, until chicken is tender. Remove from oven. Remove bouquet garni. Place pan over medium-high heat,.bring to boiling, reduce heat and allow to boil 5 to 10 minutes, until juices are reduced about ⅓. Serve with Pilaff.

PILAFF

Place second frying pan over medium-high heat at the same time you are browning the chicken. This is a double-header.

1 Large onion, minced
2½ Tablespoons unsalted
   butter, divided
1½ Cups rice

3 Cups water or chicken
   or beef stock
1 Bouquet garni
   Salt to taste

Melt 1½ tablespoons of the butter over medium-high heat and when foaming add onion and cook until transparent. Add rice and stir until each grain is covered with butter. Add water or stock, salt and bouquet garni. Bring to boiling, cover and place in oven for 20 minutes along with the chicken. Remove to serving dish. Mix in remaining butter. Cover and keep warm.

INDONESIAN CHICKEN AND RICE   Serves 8

(Nasi Goreng)

This Indonesian dish, an East Asiatic relative of Lamb Curry, is glamorous and delicious, worthy of the most elegant dinner party. Prepare the chicken and rice the day before, if desired. Serve with condiments customary with LAMB CURRY (Page 77). CELERY ROOT VINAIGRETTE (Page 121) *and* CUCUMBERS WITH YOGURT (Page 121) *are excellent with Nasi Goreng. In Indonesia, cool beer accompanies Rijsttafel, which is what Nasi Goreng is.*

1 5-7 pound roasting or
   stewing chicken. Follow
   recipe for Chicken
   Stock (Page 16)
2 Cups rice
3½ Cups chicken stock
⅓ Cup peanut oil
1½ Cups chopped onions
2 Cloves garlic, minced

1 Cup cooked shrimp
1 Cup crab meat
1 Cup cubed ham
2 Teaspoons ground coriander
1 Teaspoon ground cumin
½ Teaspoon chili powder
¼ Teaspoon mace
¼ Cup peanut butter

Remove chicken from stock. Remove skin and meat from bones and cut meat into strips. Strain stock. Wash rice and place in top of double boiler with chicken stock. Cover and cook over simmering water until rice is tender and no liquid remains. Heat oil in large skillet or dutch oven. Add onions and garlic and cook until onions are transparent, stirring. Still stirring, add rice and cook until lightly browned. Add chicken and all remaining ingredients. Mix well and heat through on low heat, making sure it does not stick and burn.

SWEDISH MEAT BALLS   3 or 4 Dozen

A tried-and-true recipe for dinners, receptions and parties. Make ahead and freeze. This recipe is similar to Prince Charles' favorite Frikadeller.

2 Slices white bread
½ Cup milk
1½ Pounds ground raw chicken or turkey
1½ Pounds ground raw veal
4 Large eggs
½ Cup *each* minced onion and minced parsley

1 Teaspoon fresh thyme leaves, or ½ teaspoon dried
2 Teaspoons salt, or to taste
Few grindings black pepper
¼ Cup Parmesan cheese
Flour for dredging
2 Tablespoons butter, or more if needed

Soak bread in milk until absorbed. Add all remaining ingredients except flour and butter. Shape into small balls, roll in flour, brown in butter on all sides. Place in baking pan or casserole. Bake in 350 degree F. oven for 15 minutes.

MEAT BALLS WITH MUSHROOMS

Saute 1 cup chopped onions in 2 tablespoons butter until transparent. Add 2 cups sliced fresh mushrooms and cook, stirring, 5 minutes longer. Arrange over meatballs in casserole and serve.

See also SWEET AND SOUR MEATBALLS (Page 10).

Mark Lanfear's

STUFFED CHICKEN BREASTS   Serves 4

Mark was Columbia River Kitchen's chef for 2 years before he began his own catering business from his stone house in Squilchuck Canyon.

The following dish is excellent served as is, but according to Mark, also good with Mornay Sauce, Brown Sauce or Diable Sauce. The Mushroom Pâté is an excellent stuffing for pork chops if you substitute thyme or sage for the tarragon; and for other meats as well. He suggests a green salad, sugar peas and boiled, dilled new potatoes as accompaniments. Topped off with a strawberry dessert.

4 Whole chicken breasts,
   skinned and boned
8 Slices Swiss cheese
   (Jarlsberg preferred)

1 Cup dry white wine
Flour and paprika for
   dusting chicken
Mushroom Pâté

Pâté may be prepared in advance and refrigerated until ready for use.

MUSHROOM PÂTÉ

1½ Cups fresh mushrooms
    chopped fine
 ½ Cup minced green onion
  2 Tablespoons butter
  2 Cloves garlic
  1 Tablespoon olive oil
 ½ Cup fine, dry bread crumbs

2 Teaspoons fresh minced
  tarragon, or 1 teaspoon,
  dried
½ Cup dry white wine
Salt and freshly ground
  pepper to taste

In frying pan over medium-high heat saute mushrooms and green onion for 3 or 4 minutes, stirring. Press in garlic juice. Add remaining ingredients. Remove from heat. Cool.

Preheat oven to 350 degrees F. In skinning and boning chicken breasts, be careful not to separate halves. Pound lightly to flatten. Divide pâté into 4 parts. With inside of chicken breasts up, place a slice of cheese in the center. Top with ¼ of the pâté. Lay on another slice of cheese. Fold sides of chicken over the pâté. Repeat with remaining breasts. Place in buttered baking dish, fold side down. Dust with flour and paprika. Pour wine into baking dish. Bake, covered, for 1½ hours.

MORNAY SAUCE: To BÉCHAMEL SAUCE (Page 152) add ¼ cup diced Gruyère and ¼ cup grated Parmesan cheese. Stir over low heat until cheese is melted. Add 2 tablespoons unsalted butter.

BROWN SAUCE: Melt 1½ tablespoons butter. Add 1½ tablespoons flour and cook, stirring, until browned. Add 2 cups hot BROWN STOCK (Page 23).

DIABLE SAUCE: Reduce ½ cup combined dry red and white wines by ⅓ over medium-high heat. Add 1 tablespoon minced shallots or green onion. Add ¾ cup Brown Sauce and 2 tablespoons butter.

LAMB DISHES

Alice Stojowski's

LAMB SHISH KEBAB — Serves 8-10

Dr. Al barbecued these delicious kebabs when he and Alice entertained friends at their Lake Chelan cabin.

1 Leg of lamb, 4 to 6 pounds, boned and cut into 2-inch cubes

Tomato chunks
Green pepper chunks
Mushrooms caps

MARINADE

½ Pound sliced onions
1 Tablespoon salt
1 Tablespoon pepper
1 Tablespoon paprika

⅔ Cup vegetable oil
½ Cup Sherry (optional)
1-3 Tablespoons ground oregano, to taste

Mix marinade ingredients. Add lamb cubes and marinate overnight. When ready to cook, place on skewers, alternating cubes with bite-size chunks of tomato, green pepper and/or mushrooms. Cook over charcoal or under broiler until crisp. Serve with rice.

LAMB CURRY — Serves 4

A glamorous party dish deserving a special setting of mellow, earthy table arrangements. Use non-matching serving pieces: wooden bowls for nuts, a lacquer bowl for the rice, assorted ceramic pots and bowls for other condiments.

Lean pork or beef may be substituted for the lamb. Leftover cooked, diced turkey or chicken can make their departure in a last burst of glory in this curry. In the case of cooked meats, omit the browning of the meat, and add with the raisins and seasonings.

2 Tablespoons butter
2 Pounds boneless lamb, cut in 1½-inch cubes
1 Cup chopped onion
½ Medium green pepper, finely chopped
½ Cup finely chopped celery
2 Cups Chicken Stock (Page 16) or equivalent, canned
1½ Tablespoons curry powder, or more to taste

¼ Teaspoon *each* ginger and turmeric
¼ Cup all-purpose flour
1 Teaspoon salt
Few grindings black pepper
½ Cup seedless raisins
¼ Cup yogurt
2 Tablespoons whipping cream
1 Teaspoon paprika
Plain Steamed Rice (Page 131)

77

In dutch oven or 6-quart heavy saucepan over high heat quickly brown lamb in butter. Remove meat and set aside. Add onion to pot and lightly brown, stirring. Add green pepper, celery and chicken stock. Return meat to pot, bring to boiling, reduce heat and simmer 15 minutes.

Mix curry powder, ginger, turmeric, flour, salt and pepper. Add enough of the stock from the pot gradually, blending well, for pouring consistency. Return to meat mixture slowly, stirring to blend. Add raisins. Cover and simmer 15 minutes longer, or until meat is tender. Remove from heat, stir in yogurt, cream and paprika. *Do not boil.*

Serve with rice and condiments in separate bowls. Suggestions: flaked coconut, green grapes, peanuts, chutneys (Major Grey's is good) including homemade, chopped chives or green onions, candied ginger, bacon bits, preserved kumquats, sliced cucumbers, cut tomatoes, grated hard-cooked eggs, marinated mushrooms.

To serve: Spoon rice on plates, top with curried meat sauce, sprinkle with any or all the condiments.

Suggested desserts: APRICOT BABA RING (Page 169) or CHOCOLATE BAVARIAN (Page 157).

BRAISED LAMB SHANKS   Serves 4

Lamb shanks are few and far between in the meat markets, so when you see them, grab them! Here's a less expensive cut of meat you can convert to a mouth-watering dish.

4 **Lamb shanks**	3 **Tablespoons butter or**
½ **Cup flour**	**vegetable oil**
1 **Teaspoon salt**	4 **Cups canned or fresh**
Few grindings black pepper	**tomatoes, pureed**
1 **Cup chopped onions**	1 **Bay leaf**

Dust lamb shanks in flour, salt and pepper mixture. Melt butter in skillet over medium-high heat. Stir in onions and cook for 2 or 3 minutes, until transparent. Remove from skillet. Add more butter or oil to skillet if it seems dry. Brown lamb shanks on all sides. Transfer to dutch oven. Add tomatoes and bay leaf and taste for seasoning. Bring to boiling, reduce heat, cover and simmer 3 hours, or until lamb shanks are tender. *Or* bake, covered, in 325 degree F. oven.

FISH & SEAFOOD

STEAMED CLAMS

It was always worth a trip to Seattle's Pike Place Market just to see the piles of butter clams when they're in season. But now Wenatchee's The Dolphin Express (formerly Fisherman Ken's) has water tanks mounded with living and breathing clams, oysters and lobsters. Grab a few pounds of clams and have a feast.

2 Pounds butter clams per person, or more, depending on individual capacities

Cornmeal
Melted butter

Scrub clams thoroughly. Place in large pan, cover with cold water and sprinkle with cornmeal. Clams "clean themselves" via this process. Let stand several hours or overnight. Rinse thoroughly.

Place in steamer or large kettle with 1 cup of water over high heat. Bring to boiling, turn heat to low and allow to steam, covered, 10 minutes or until clams open. Some of them may be late bloomers, so leave them alone until you're ready for the second round. Place in large individual bowls with melted butter in individual dishes for dipping. Pour a mug of clam nectar for each person. Serve with crusty rolls and a green salad.

Discard clams that do not open.

COQUILLES SAINT JACQUES   Serves 2-3

The most delicious version of this dish I've ever tasted was served in the restaurant of the ancient Chateau d'Isenbourg, Rouffach, near Colmar during our gastronomic tour of France. Served with legumes and rice, this is my remembrance of it.

1 Pound scallops
2 Teaspoons minced shallots or onions, preferably Walla Walla Sweets
Pinch of salt

Dash of white pepper
½ Cup dry white wine
½ Cup heavy cream
Shredded carrot and cabbage for garnish

In saucepan combine scallops, shallots or onion, seasonings and wine. Bring to boiling, reduce heat and simmer, covered, for 3 minutes. Remove scallops and keep warm. Return liquid to boiling and reduce ½. Add cream. Boil until reduced to consistency of syrup. To serve, spoon scallops into serving dish or individual plates. Spoon sauce over. Sprinkle with barest shreds of carrot and cabbage.

FRIED OYSTERS
Serves 2

Live oysters are available in Wenatchee, so give yourself and your family a treat. Of course, the shucked ones in jars will do. Pick the size you prefer.

1 Pint fresh oysters, drained	Cracker or dry bread
2 Eggs, fork beaten	crumbs
2 Teaspoons cold water	4 Tablespoons butter, or
	more as needed

To open oysters in the shell, place on baking pan in 400 degree F. oven for 15 minutes. This will cause them to open just enough for you to wedge in a screwdriver to pry them open the rest of the way. Be sure to save the juices. Mix beaten egg with water.

Dip oysters in beaten egg, then in cracker or bread crumbs. Meanwhile, melt butter in heavy skillet over medium-high heat. Saute oysters to a nice golden brown on each side—about 3 minutes altogether.

Serve with COLE SLAW (Page 36), a buttered crusty roll, and a chilled bottle of Johannisberg Riesling.

Jean Ludwick's
OYSTERS CASINO
Serves 2

If you love oysters, and you don't have a lot of time on your hands, make this delicious dish. Wonderful as an appetizer.

1 Pint fresh oysters, drained	1 Teaspoon lemon juice
3 Slices bacon, cut fine	½ Teaspoon salt
4 Tablespoons chopped onion	½ Teaspoon pepper
2 Tablespoons chopped	½ Teaspoon Worcestershire
green pepper	sauce
2 Tablespoons chopped celery	2 Drops hot pepper sauce

In frying pan over medium heat fry bacon until crisp. Remove from pan with slotted spoon. Add onion, green pepper and celery and stir-fry until just tender. Drain fat. Add remaining ingredients except oysters, and mix well. Preheat oven to 350 degrees F.

Arrange drained oysters in buttered baking dish (glass pie plate will do), and spread bacon mixture over oysters. *Or,* if you have oyster shells, place an oyster in each shell, arrange in a baking pan half-filled with rock salt, and bake 20 to 25 minutes.

SAUTEED FILET OF SOLE
Serves 4

I use the following simple recipe for all kinds of fish: halibut, sole, trout, salmon, red snapper, petrale sole, Greenland turbot, etc.

It is important, in order to achieve the utmost flavor, to brown the butter. Be careful not to burn.

4 Large filets of sole
½ Cup (1 cube) butter, preferably unsalted

Salt and freshly ground pepper to taste

In heavy frying pan over medium-high heat melt the butter. Watch carefully and when it turns a light golden brown quickly add the fish filets. Sprinkle with salt and pepper. Allow to lightly brown, and turn. Cook only 2 or 3 minutes in all. Remove to warm serving dish or plates. Pour pan juices over. Garnish with lemon wedges.

FILET OF SOLE AMANDINE: Brown blanched, slivered almonds in the butter in which fish was cooked. Spoon over sole and serve.

BAKED SALMON
Serves 6-8

In my experience, there isn't an easier way of preparing salmon than the following method. Moist and delicious, I've served it for countless dinners. A truly Northwest experience with a fresh cooked vegetable such as green beans julienne; tiny boiled, buttered new potatoes sprinkled with chopped fresh dill, cilantro or parsley; herbed French bread; a tossed green salad with good olive oil and vinegar dressing; and for dessert, wild blackberry or apple pie with whipped cream.

1 8-pound King or Silver Salmon
1 Small onion, sliced paper thin
Sprig of fresh fennel or a sprinkling of fennel seeds, if desired
2 Tablespoons butter, preferably unsalted

2-3 Bacon slices
Salt and freshly ground pepper
½ Cup melted unsalted butter
3 Tablespoons minced parsley or snipped fennel
Garnish: Lemon wedges, olives, artichoke hearts, cherry tomatoes

Scrape salmon, if necessary, to remove all scales. Remove fins. Wash thoroughly. Remove head and tail or not, as desired. Pat dry. Season inside of fish with salt and pepper. Fill with onion slices, a sprig or sprinkling of fennel and distribute bits of butter throughout. Place bacon slices on top and wrap completely in aluminum foil. All of this preparation may be done a day in advance.

81

When ready, preheat oven to 325 degrees F. Bake one hour or more, until done. Test by opening foil and carefully probing the thickest part of the fish at the backbone with a fork. Meat should be flaky and pink. Do not overcook.

To serve, remove salmon to platter on which you have arranged a bed of greens. Discard bacon. Carefully remove top skin and pour over the top the melted butter mixed with the minced parsley. Decorate platter with suggested garnish, or your own innovation. Serve with REMOULADE DRESSING (Page 47).

The Kintners'

BARBECUED SALMON
Serves 6

When the Jacobsons and Rich Congdon hosted a riverfront gathering, Bob Kintner, with the help of kibitzers, presided at the barbecue. Melt-in-your-mouth Westport King Salmon was the pièce de resistance to which Bob applied a sauce their family has enjoyed for 25 years—a creation of sister-in-law Christine of Port Townsend. Roasted ears of freshly picked corn gathered the same afternoon in the Jim Morans' corn patch, raw vegetable and molded salads, fresh fruits, cold beer and soft drinks rounded out a memorable feast.

1 6-pound King Salmon	2 Tablespoons paprika
½ Cup (1 cube) butter	Freshly ground pepper
1 Teaspoon lemon juice	Garlic salt or powder
Sprinkling of Accent	Minced parsley

Filet fish. Using a sharp knife, remove fins. Cut through flesh along backbone from tail to head. Cut flesh away from bone on each side. Lift off filets in one piece, one on each side. (Freeze bone and trimmings for Court Bouillon). Melt butter, add remaining ingredients and mix well.

Make a tray of heavy aluminum foil, slightly larger than the salmon. Turn up edges of foil so sauce and juices won't drip on coals. Place fish skin side down on foil over moderately hot charcoal fire. Baste well with sauce. Cover with hood. Cook fish until it flakes—about 30 to 40 minutes. If your grill has no hood make a wire dome to fit grill and cover with foil.

Judy Jensen's
CANNED SALMON
Cut fresh salmon filets to fit ½ pint or pint jars, roll an[...]
leaving one inch clearance from top. Add ¼ teaspoon salt to each ½
pint. Screw on lid. Process in pressure cooker at 10 pounds for 100
minutes. As many as 25 jars can be stacked in a large pressure cooker.

Voltaire Bousquet's
POACHED SALMON   Serves 10

*Voltaire Bousquet is one of the many North Central Washington fish-
ermen who heads for Westport, Ocean Shores, Ilwaco, La Push or
other coastal points when the salmon begin congregating in May and
June for the annual migration up Washington streams and rivers to
the spawning grounds.*

*Use a fish poacher if you have one, but any container, such as a
roaster, will do if the salmon is wrapped in cheesecloth so that it can
be lifted out of the container without losing its shape. Allow the ends
of cheesecloth to hang out over the top of the pan for easy grasping.*

1 **Whole 9 or 10-pound King
or Silver Salmon,**
½ **Cup melted,
unsalted butter**

3 **Tablespoons minced parsley
or cilantro
Lemon or lime wedges,
Artichoke hearts for garnish**

COURT BOUILLON
4 **Cups water**
2 **Cups dry white wine**
¼ **Cup wine vinegar**
3 **Onions, thickly sliced**
2 **Carrots, cut in
1-inch chunks**
4 **Celery stalks with light
green leaves, cut in
1-inch pieces**

4 **Parsley sprigs**
2 **Garlic cloves**
2 **Bay leaves**
1 **Teaspoon *each* finely cut
fresh tarragon and thyme,
or ½ teaspoon dried**
1 **Tablespoon salt**
10 **Peppercorns**

Place all ingredients except salmon in medium saucepan and cook until vegetables are tender. Strain. After fish has poached, strain again
and freeze for future seafood dishes. You now have Court Bouillon.

Place fish in poacher or other container. Pour in Court Bouillon and add enough water to cover the fish by one inch. Bring to simmering over medium heat and poach about 30 minutes, or until fish flakes at the thickest part when tested with a fork. Do not allow water to boil. Do not overcook. Lift salmon from container and place on surface to drain. Carefully remove skin (and head, if desired).

Transfer to serving board or platter on which you have arranged a bed of greens. Pour melted butter over salmon. Sprinkle with minced fresh parsley or cilantro. Garnish with wedges of lemon and/or lime and artichoke hearts. Accompany with CUCUMBERS AND SOUR CREAM or YOGURT (Page 121) or NAMASU (Page 122); boiled new potatoes sprinkled with chopped fresh dill; and fresh asparagus in season. Remoulade Dressing is a good accompaniment.

SENSUOUS SALMON

Yep, that's what the nation's leading fashion publication calls this combination: Cold poached salmon with homemade herbed mayonnaise and a garniture of crisp, red radishes and cucumbers. Add a chilled bottle of Pouilly Fuisse or Chablis.

EGG DISHES & SAUCES

THE FRESH EGG TEST

To test for freshness, place the egg in cold water just to cover. If it lies flat, it is fresh. If it tilts slightly, use it for baking. It it stands straight up, forget it.

THE PERFECT POACHED EGG

The perfect poached egg is elliptical, the white masking the yolk completely. This cannot be achieved with a stale egg, because the white will disintegrate and trail off in the poaching water, leaving the yolk exposed. So be sure your eggs are fresh.

You will need a skillet full of gently simmering water to which vinegar has been added—about one tablespoonful to a quart of water. The vinegar helps to keep the white intact about the yolk. Have available also a pan of hot water in which to dip the egg after it has poached, in order to remove the vinegar.

Puncture the broad end of the egg with a needle. Place the eggs in the simmering water, 2 at a time, and roll them back and forth 8 or 10 times. This helps the white to coagulate. Remove with a slotted spoon.

Now break the eggs on the side of the skillet and lower carefully into the simmering water. Poach for 3 or 4 minutes, maintaining the water at a gentle simmer.

Remove egg with a slotted spoon and dip into the pan or bowl of hot water. Drain and serve on a slice of hot buttered toast or English muffin.

THE PERFECT OMELET

The eggs for a perfect omelet must be very fresh. The pan for the perfect omelet should be about 7 inches in diameter, with sloping sides.

For each omelet break 3 large eggs in a bowl. Add 1 tablespoon water, ¼ teaspoon salt and a few grindings of pepper. Beat vigorously with a fork just enough to mix yolks and whites. If you overbeat, the omelet will not be fluffy.

Set omelet pan over high heat and let it get hot enough so that when you sprinkle a few drops of water on the pan they will jump around and disappear. Add 2 tablespoons butter, preferably unsalted, tilting pan to cover well the sides and bottom.

85

When foam begins to subside and butter is turning golden in color, pour in the beaten eggs. They should hit the pan sizzling.

Working fast, make 8 to 10 quick circular motions with a fork flat on the bottom of the pan, to raise layers of fluffiness. At the same time shake pan to and fro roughly, and continue the shaking process.

When omelet has begun to set and looks glossy, a matter of a few seconds, let it rest for 2 or 3 seconds, and test for rolling by tilting the pan and lifting the outer edges with a fork. (This is the time to add the filling, if you are using one, distributing it over the surface of the omelet).

If the omelet comes away from the pan easily, hold the tilted pan over a heated plate and with the aid of the fork roll it over onto the plate. The whole process should take just over a minute. Serve immediately.

Roslyn Cafe's
GREEN PEPPER OMELET
Serves 2

One weekend, enroute from Seattle to Wenatchee, we stopped in the tiny, picturesque old mining town of Roslyn and ordered an omelet in the Roslyn Cafe. Chef-owner Kim McJury told us she'd lived on Lake Union in Seattle when she and her husband visited Roslyn, and decided this was where they wanted to live. When the old building in which they are housed came on the market, they decided to buy it and go into the restaurant business "even though I'm not much of a cook". Don't let that modest talk fool you.

FILLING
½ Cup tomato sauce
1 Cup canned tomatoes
1 4-ounce can mild
  green chilies
2 Cloves garlic
  Hot red peppers (to taste)

⅓ Teaspoon cumin
1½ Cups grated sharp
  cheddar cheese
4 Whole green chilies
  Sour cream for garnish

Place all ingredients in blender except the cheese, the whole green chilies and sour cream. Liquefy. Prepare omelets and fill each with some of the blender mixture, ½ cup grated cheese and 2 whole chilies. Sprinkle with remainder of cheese. Place lid on pan, steam for a minute to raise omelet and melt cheese. Place on serving plate. Garnish with sour cream.

Kim makes a 2-egg omelet for this dish. She used 2 hot red peppers for each batch of filling. You could make one large omelet and halve when serving.

Carmen's
SCRAMBLED EGGS AND MUSHROOMS   Serves 4

The Boletus, Morel, Chanterelle and other edible mushrooms are found in the forests, hills and meadows of North Central Washington. But patches, like the blackberry, aren't noised about. We have found Boletus at Lake Wenatchee in late September following the rains. During 1980 I found them under our fir trees right here in Wenatchee.

When my brother brings home a bucketful of Boletus, his wife prepares their favorite breakfast.

6 Strips bacon, diced	8 Eggs, beaten
1 Onion, minced	
2 Cups diced Boletus mush- rooms, or other edible mushrooms	

Cook bacon until crisp. Add onions and cook until transparent and golden. Add mushrooms and heat thoroughly. Add beaten eggs, stirring over low heat until set.

ASPARAGUS EGGS BENEDICT   Serves 4

A wonderful luncheon, supper or brunch dish. Garnish with parlsey or water cress and tomato; or papaya and pineapple spears.

20 Spears asparagus (4 or 5 per person)	4 English muffins, or 4 slices French bread,
2 Tablespoons butter	toasted and buttered
½-1 Pound Canadian bacon or boneless cooked ham cut 1/8 to ¼-inch thick	4 Large eggs, poached 1¼ Cups Mustard Hollandaise

Cut away tough parts of asparagus stems and save for stockpot. Peel stalks about ⅔ up from base. Place spears in large saucepan. Add 1 cup water and ¼ teaspoon salt. Bring to boiling, reduce heat and steam, covered, for 10 minutes or until stems are just tender when pierced, Remove from heat. Drain. Save water for stockpot.

Brown ham or bacon in butter. Poach eggs. Toast muffins or bread, and butter while eggs are poaching. Place muffins or bread on serving plates. Place ham or bacon on the toast, and poached eggs on the ham. If muffins are used, place ham on thicker portion and use thin slice as extra toast. Place asparagus on the side. Spoon 2 or 3 tablespoons Mustard Hollandaise over all.

BLENDER HOLLANDAISE (1¼ cups)

½ Cup melted butter   ¼ Teaspoon salt
4 Egg yolks   Dash hot pepper sauce
2 Tablespoons lemon juice

Melt butter until bubbly. Place eggs yolks, lemon juice, salt and pepper sauce in blender. Turn on and off to mix. Turn on blender to high and dribble butter into mixture until thickened. The butter *must* be bubbly or the sauce will not thicken. Hold over warm water until ready to serve. If too thick, add 1 tablespoon hot water. Serve with poached eggs, artichokes, asparagus, broccoli, poached fish.

MUSTARD HOLLANDAISE

Add 1 tablespoon or more prepared mustard (French or domestic) to above recipe.

HAM AND EGG SOUFFLE   Serves 4

A versatile luncheon, supper or brunch dish. Sauteed pork sausages, crabmeat, leftover turkey or chicken, or shrimp may be substituted for the ham. Prepare the day before and pop in the oven when you come home from work. Serve with a green salad or fruit.

8 Slices bread, buttered and crusts removed
4 Slices sharp cheddar cheese, ¼-inch thick
1 Cup chopped ham, or other meat or shellfish
1 Tablespoon chopped green pepper
1 Tablespoon minced onion or chives

4 Large eggs
2 Cups milk
1 Teaspoon dry mustard
½ Teaspoon salt
Few grindings black pepper
1 Tablespoon minced parsley

Place 4 slices of bread in flat buttered baking dish. Place the 4 slices of cheese on the bread and cover with remaining 4 slices of bread. Sprinkle with ham, green pepper and onion. Mix eggs, milk, mustard, salt and pepper. Pour over bread and refrigerate overnight.

Next day bring to room temperature. Sprinkle with parsley. Bake at 350 degrees F. for 45 minutes, or until custard is set.

CRAB QUICHE
Serves 7

The recipe for Columbia River Kitchen's popular Crab Quiche used the hot-water pastry developed when Florence Orndoff was Chief Baker. However, the BASIC PIE CRUST (Page 181) *may be used.*

PASTRY

1 Cup unsifted, unbleached all-purpose flour
¼ Cup vegetable shortening or lard
¼ Cup (½ cube) butter

½ Teaspoon sugar
1/8 Teaspoon salt
½ Teaspoon vinegar
¼ Cup hot water

Work together until crumbly the flour, shortening and butter, sugar and salt. Mix vinegar and hot water and add, stirring into a ball. Refrigerate until firm enough to roll. When ready to bake, follow instructions for PREBAKED PIE SHELL (Page 182), using a 9-inch deep dish glass pie pan.

FILLING

¼ Cup finely cut green onion tops or chives
¼ Cup minced parsley
1 Cup Dungeness or Alaska King crabmeat
1 Cup shredded Swiss cheese

4 Large eggs
2 Cups light cream
½ Teaspoon salt
1/8 Teaspoon white pepper
¼ Teaspoon nutmeg
Paprika

Preheat oven to 300 degrees F. Sprinkle bottom of baked pie shell with green onion tops or chives and parsley. Layer evenly with crabmeat and then with shredded cheese. Beat eggs with cream, salt, pepper and nutmeg. Pour over cheese. Sprinkle with paprika. Bake 40 minutes, or until center is set and quiche is golden in color. Serve hot, warm or cold.

OK, DON'T JUST SIT THERE

Did you know that sitting in front of the TV or sleeping too much might be a good way to get gall or kidney stones? The experts say that bone calcium content is based on muscle pull and weight bearing and if you don't get either the calcium is absorbed in the blood stream. So where does that leave your bones?

VARIATION

MEXICAN QUICHE: Omit crabmeat. Sprinkle baked crust with onion tops or chives and parsley. Dot with 8 ounces diced cream cheese. Layer two 4-ounce cans of drained and finely chopped green chilies over cream cheese. Layer with 1 cup shredded cheddar, Swiss or Jack cheese. Pour egg and cream mixture over cheese. Sprinkle with paprika. Bake 40 minutes in 300 degree F. oven, or until center is set and quiche is golden in color.

MUSHROOM-ZUCCHINI FRITTATA   Serves 7

Columbia River Kitchen customers were always asking for the Frittata recipes!

1 Cup sliced fresh mushrooms	1/8 Teaspoon white pepper
1 Cup finely chopped onion	1½ Cups crumbled whole
1 Cup finely chopped celery	grain bread
1 Cup thinly sliced,	8 Ounces cream cheese,
unpared zucchini	cut in ½-inch cubes
⅔ Cup finely chopped	1 Cup shredded sharp
green pepper	cheddar cheese, plus
1 Teaspoon minced garlic	¼ cup for garnish
1 Tablespoon vegetable oil	1 Cup cubed medium
5 Large eggs	cheddar cheese
⅓ Cup light cream	½ Cup minced parsley
¼ Teaspoon salt	plus extra for garnish

Preheat oven to 350 degrees F. In large skillet, stir-fry in vegetable oil until crisp-tender the mushrooms, onion, celery, green pepper, zucchini and garlic. *Or* omit oil and quickly steam in ¼ cup water in covered saucepan until just limp. Drain. Cool. Save water for stock pot or drink it.

Beat eggs with cream, salt and pepper. Place crumbled bread in large bowl. Mix in the shredded sharp cheese, the cubed cheddar cheese and parsley. Mix in the cooled vegetables, the egg mixture, and finally, the cubed cream cheese.

Pour into well-buttered 9-inch deep-dish glass pie plate. Sprinkle with cheddar cheese and parsley. Bake 35 to 45 minutes, or until set in the center and lightly browned. Cool 10 minutes before cutting.

VARIATIONS

SAUSAGE-POTATO FRITTATA   Serves 7

½ Cup sliced fresh mushrooms
½ Cup finely chopped onion
½ Cup finely chopped celery
1½ Cups shredded cabbage
½ Teaspoon minced garlic
1 Tablespoon vegetable oil
5 Large eggs
⅓ Cup light cream
¼ Teaspoon salt
1/8 Teaspoon white pepper
1 Cup crumbled whole-grain bread

1 Cup cooked, diced potatoes
2 Cups sliced, cooked Swedish, German or Polish Sausage
1 Cup cubed medium cheddar cheese
1 Cup shredded sharp cheddar cheese, plus ¼ cup for garnish
½ Teaspoon caraway seed
½ Cup minced parsley, plus ¼ cup for garnish

Follow procedure for Mushroom Zucchini Frittata, adding potatoes and sausage to crumbled bread with other ingredients.

MEXICAN FRITTATA   Serves 7

1 Tablespoon olive oil
½ Cup finely chopped onion
½ Cup finely chopped green pepper
½ Pound lean ground beef
½ Pound lean ground pork
1 Teaspoon minced garlic
1 Teaspoon ground cumin
½ Teaspoon chili powder
1 4-ounce can green chilies, chopped and drained
5 Large eggs
⅓ Cup light cream

¼ Teaspoon salt
1/8 Teaspoon white pepper
1½ Cups crumbled whole-grain bread
1 Cup shredded sharp cheddar cheese, plus ¼ cup for garnish
1 Cup cubed medium cheddar cheese
8 Ounces cream cheese, cut in ½-inch cubes
½ Cup minced parsley, plus extra for garnish

Preheat oven to 350 degrees F. In large skillet over high heat, stir-fry onions and green pepper in olive oil for 2 minutes. Remove with slotted spoon. Add the meats and garlic and cook for 3 or 4 minutes, reduce heat to medium and continue cooking for 15 minutes, stirring occasionally, until meat is well browned. Drain excess fat. Stir in cumin, chili powder and chilies.

Beat eggs with cream, salt and pepper. Place crumbled bread in large bowl. Mix in the shredded sharp cheese, the cubed cheddar cheese and parsley. Stir in the onion and green pepper, the meat mixture, the egg mixture and cubed cream cheese.

Pour into well-buttered 9-inch deep-dish pie plate. Sprinkle with cheddar cheese and parsley. Bake 35 to 45 minutes, or until set in the center and lightly browned. Cool 10 minutes before cutting.

ITALIAN FRITTATA: Substitute 2½ cups LASAGNA MEAT SAUCE (Page 94) for the beef, pork, chili powder, cumin and chilies.

PASTA DISHES & SAUCES

FETTUCINE ALFREDO
Serves 4

*Pastas are definitely **in**. So here's a delicious, fashionable dish you can prepare in a flash.*

1 Pound fettucine noodles, cooked according to package directions, drained. If you are using fresh fettucini cook in boiling salted water about 10 minutes, until just tender. Drain.	**½ Cup (1 cube) butter, preferably unsalted** **½ Cup grated Parmesan cheese** **¾ Cup grated Swiss cheese** **½ Cup whipping cream** **Few grindings black pepper** **Minced parsley**

In medium saucepan over medium heat melt the butter. Add fettucine and grated Swiss cheese and blend well. Add cream and pepper. Turn into serving dish. Sprinkle with Parmesan cheese and parsley. Serve immediately.

VARIATION

FETTUCINE WITH PESTO SAUCE: Cook fettucini noodles or other pasta. Mix with PESTO SAUCE (Page 18).

See also HOMEMADE NOODLES (Page 25)

LASAGNA
Serves 8

This terrific dish is worthy of a party, and may be assembled in advance, refrigerated or frozen and baked when needed. Add a green salad, a sourdough roll, a glass of good Chianti, California Cabernet Sauvignon or Zinfandel, and you have a feast.

The Meat Sauce may be used with a vast array of pasta: spaghetti, fettucini, canneloni, manicotti, etc. Pour it on a bun for a Sloppy Joe. Try it in pocket bread for a tasty sandwich. Substitute cumin and chili powder for the basil and oregano for a Mexican accent. Make it in double and triple quantities when there's a good buy on ground beef or pork and freeze.

MEAT SAUCE

1 Pound lean ground chuck
1 Pound lean ground pork
3 Cloves garlic, minced
1 Cup chopped onion
½ Cup chopped celery
1 Teaspoon salt
Few grindings black pepper
½ Teaspoon dried oregano,
   or 1 teaspoon fresh

1½ Teaspoons dried basil, or
   3 teaspoons fresh
½ Cup minced parsley
4 Cups canned or fresh
   tomatoes, pureed
2 6-ounce cans tomato paste

In large frying pan or dutch oven over medium-high heat cook beef and pork, onion, garlic and celery until meat is well browned. Add seasonings and herbs and mix well. Add tomatoes and tomato paste. Bring to boiling, reduce heat, cover and simmer for 2 hours or longer until mixture is very thick, stirring frequently. Remove from heat. Skim off all fat.

LASAGNA

¾ Pound lasagna noodles
4 Quarts boiling water
1 Tablespoon salt
1 Pound mozzarella cheese,
   thinly sliced

1 Pound ricotta cheese,
   cream cheese or
   drained cottage cheese
1 Cup grated Parmesan cheese
   Ripe olives and minced
   parsley for garnish

While meat sauce is simmering cook noodles in large saucepan in boiling salted water for 10 minutes or until just tender, but not too soft. Drain well.

To assemble, cover bottom of 9 x 13 baking dish with ⅓ of the Meat Sauce. Layer with ½ the noodles. Top with ½ the mozzarella and ½ the Parmesan cheeses. Repeat with another third of the Meat Sauce, the remainder of the noodles and the cream cheese, ricotta or cottage cheese. Finish with the remainder of the Meat Sauce and a layer of mozzarella. Sprinkle with remainder of the Parmesan cheese and the minced parsley. Garnish with olives and parsley.

Cover with foil and bake at 375 degrees F. for 25 minutes. Remove foil. Bake 30 minutes longer, until bubbly and a nice golden brown. Cool 15 minutes before serving. Cut in squares.

ITALIAN CRÊPES: Fill CRÊPES (Page 66) with Lasagna Meat Sauce. Roll up. Cover with MARINARA SAUCE (Page 96). Sprinkle with Parmesan cheese and minced parsley. Garnish with green stuffed or ripe olives and slivered pimientos. Bake uncovered at 350 degrees F until sauce bubbles and crêpes and sauce are golden in color, about 30 minutes.

Beverly Kemp's
MANICOTTI Serves 4

This is the most delicious Manicotti tested. Crêpes may be substituted for the purchased manicotti shells (Page 66).

MEAT SAUCE
1 Pound lean ground beef
½ Pound pork sausage
½ Cup chopped onion
   Salt and freshly ground
   black pepper to taste
1 Teaspoon *each* dried thyme
   leaves, rosemary and basil,
   or twice as much, fresh

½ Cup Sauterne or
   Cream Sherry
1 No. 2½ can solid
   pack tomatoes (3½ cups)
1 6-ounce can tomato paste
1 Cup sliced,
   fresh mushrooms

Brown meat in large skillet over medium-high heat. Spoon off fat. Add remaining ingredients, bring to boiling, reduce heat and simmer, covered, while preparing stuffing.

STUFFING
1 Cup cooked spinach
1 Cup cottage cheese
1 Egg
½ Cup Parmesan cheese
1 Tablespoon dried basil, or
   2 tablespoons fresh, minced

1 Clove garlic, minced
   Salt and freshly ground
   black pepper to taste
8 Manicotti shells

Preheat oven to 375 degrees F. Mix all ingredients and stuff uncooked manicotti shells. (If you are using crepes, place ¼ cup stuffing on each crepe. Roll up). Place in buttered 9 x 13 baking dish. Cover with Meat Sauce. Top with Garnish. Cover with foil and bake 1¼ hours.

GARNISH
½ Cup grated American or
   Parmesan Cheese
½ Cup minced parsley

Ripe olives and/or
pimiento strips

ITALIAN SPAGHETTI AND MEAT BALLS   Serves 8

Add a green salad with a good olive oil based FRENCH DRESSING
(Page 43), *a crusty roll and a bottle of Chianti Classico or Vino Rosso.*

1 Recipe Swedish Meat
  Balls (Page 75). Substitute
  lean ground pork for
  raw chicken or turkey.
2 Tablespoons olive oil

1 Recipe Marinara Sauce
1½ Pounds spaghetti
½ Cup Parmesan cheese
½ Cup minced parsley

Heat oil in large skillet over medium-high heat and brown meat balls
on all sides. Place in dutch oven or heavy sauce pan. Cover with
Marinara Sauce. Bring to boiling, reduce heat and simmer 30
minutes, stirring frequently to prevent sticking and burning.

Cook spaghetti according to manufacturer's directions on package.
Drain in colander and rinse with hot water. Drain completely.

To serve, place spaghetti on large heated platter. Spoon over the
MeatBalls and Sauce. Sprinkle with Parmesan cheese and minced
parsley.

MARINARA SAUCE (5 cups)

3 Tablespoons olive oil
2 Garlic cloves, minced
½ Cup chopped onion
½ Cup chopped celery
½ Cup chopped green pepper
1 Cup sliced fresh mushrooms
½ Cup minced parsley
1 Teaspoon sugar
1 Teaspoon salt
  Few grindings black pepper

1 Teaspoon dried oregano, or
  2 teaspoons fresh, minced
1 Teaspoon dried basil, or
  2 teaspoons fresh, minced
1 Bay leaf
3 Cups canned or fresh,
  pureed tomatoes
1 6-ounce can tomato paste
1 Cup water

Heat oil in large skillet over medium-high heat. Add garlic, onions,
celery, green pepper and mushrooms and cook for 6 or 7 minutes, stirring. Add all remaining ingredients. Bring to boiling, reduce heat and
simmer 20 minutes. Remove bay leaf. Taste for seasoning.

VARIATION

SPAGHETTI WITH MEAT SAUCE: Top cooked spaghetti with
LASAGNA MEAT SAUCE (Page 94), Parmesan cheese and minced
parlsey.

GAME DISHES & ACCOMPANIMENTS

Loma Yeager's
BEAR PAWS KIT CARSON (Recipe not tested)

Loma Yeager was President of the Heritage Society of the Columbia when she submitted this recipe for our Pioneer collection.

According to Loma, Indians taught early settlers to cook the front paws of bears. Although an oversupply of wild game in our national parks could make it possible to purchase this delicacy in specialty shops, Loma confesses she is not curious enough to seek out such a specialty shop.

She notes that it is believed the Chinese of Honan Province also favor bear paws.

1½ **Pounds skinned bear paws**	1 **Large onion, chopped**
1 **Quart vinegar**	2 **Carrots, sliced**
1 **Bouquet garni (bay leaf,**	1 **Quart beef stock**
thyme and parsley)	½ **Teaspoon cayenne**
4 **Strips bacon**	1 **Cup currant jelly**
2 **Slices smoked ham**	

Marinate meat in vinegar and bouquet garni in refrigerator for 5 days. In a deep pot fry bacon slightly. Add ham, bear paws, vegetables, stock and enough water to cover meat. Simmer for 8 hours, adding more beef stock if needed. Slice. Add cayenne and serve with currant jelly.

THE SMOKE HOUSE

I remember mouthwateringly the walk-in smokehouse on the Hobart farm. Graced at its entrance by a wild yellow plum tree, its interior was steeped in the fragrance of years of hams, bacons and sausages curing as they hung from the rafters above the smouldering alderwood fire.

97

SWEET AND SOUR ELK, DEER OR MOOSE

This recipe from Ruth Shutt brought back memories of moose grazing in wetlands near Anchorage, Alaska.

2-3 Pounds meat, cut in bite-
    size pieces
1 Large green pepper,
    cut in strips
2 Cups diced celery
1 10½-ounce can
    beef bouillon

2 Cups crushed pineapple
5 Tablespoons soy sauce
¼ Cup sugar
½ Cup corn syrup
¼ Cup vinegar
5 Tablespoons cornstarch
½ Cup water

Brown meat in small amount of oil, and cook until tender. Meanwhile, in medium saucepan cook green pepper and celery in a little oil for 3 or 4 minutes. Add all remaining ingredients except cornstarch and water. Simmer 10 minutes. Mix cornstarch and water, stir into sauce and cook slowly until thick, stirring. Add meat and serve on rice or noodles.

BOILED OR JELLIED MOOSE NOSE

This recipe from a hunter has not been tested.

Clean one fresh moose nose by skinning or dipping in scalding water and scraping. Remove all hair. Dice meat in small pieces. Cover with water. Add salt and pepper to taste, and 2 or 3 cloves of garlic. Boil until tender. Pour in shallow baking dish. Chill and cut in squares. Serve.

"It's a wise hunter who deadens his daytime scent by hanging his jacket in the evening smoke of his campfire".

ROAST QUAIL OR PHEASANT

One hilariously unforgettable evening in May I dined on roast quail and cherries at a sidewalk cafe in Cannes, in the company of Peggy Kells, and June and the late Frank Taylor.

My father was a bird hunter, so roast quail and pheasant were bonanzas we enjoyed now and then on the Hobart farm. (I can remember his bagging 4 quail with one blast of his shotgun into an apple tree in our front yard one winter day.)

Not so in my immediate family. No one can bear to shoot a bird! However, one day on Chatham Hill our old mother cat, perhaps sensing the lack, brought a beautiful plump quail to the kitchen and deposited it at my feet.

1 Quail Stuffing of a few mushrooms, chopped onion and bread crumbs seasoned with a sprinkling of thyme ½ Cup Chicken Stock (Page 16)	¼ Cup dry red wine 1 Bay leaf 1 *Each* chopped green onion, carrot and celery 1 Tablespoon softened butter 1 Tablespoon flour

Pluck feathers from bird and clean. Salt and pepper cavity and stuff. Sew cavity closed.

Brown bird in bacon drippings and butter in heavy skillet. Add chicken stock, wine, bay leaf and the vegetables. Simmer 30 minutes covered, or until tender. Remove bird and bay leaf from pan. Mix softened butter and flour, thin with sauce from the pan, and add to pan juices, stirring until thickened. To serve, spoon sauce over bird.

Accompany with wild rice, a salad of grapefruit, avocado and mandarin oranges vinaigrette and Pinot Chardonnay or White Burgundy.

Judy Jensen's

ELEPHANT STEW (Not tested)

Cut one elephant into bite-sized pieces. This will take about 2 months. Cover with brown gravy and cook over kerosene fire for four weeks at 465 degrees. If more than 3,800 guests are expected, add two rabbits. But do this only if absolutely necessary, as most people don't like to find hare in their stew.

Matt Burger's

ROAST WILD DUCK

Matt Burger, Chef at Wenatchee Center, prepared wild duck as follows: Stuff with a mixture of boiled wild rice, chopped green onion, chopped bacon, salt and pepper. Baste with melted butter, sprinkle with salt and pepper. Place in baking pan. Pour over orange juice. Roast 1 hour and 15 minutes at 350 degrees F.

Helen Welty's

ROAST WILD DUCK

The late Joe Welty was a hunter, and what Helen did with the ducks was marvelous.

If ducks are frozen, thaw completely by submerging in water to which dry wine or tarragon vinegar has been added. Soak overnight. This helps tenderize, and lessens the gamey taste.

Dry thoroughly and rub with garlic butter and thyme inside and out. Let stand 2 or 3 hours. Wrap in foil. Roast breast down 3 hours in 250 degree F oven, or until tender, opening foil wrapper occasionally to baste with sherry.

Chill thoroughly before slicing meat if it is to be served with cocktails. Otherwise, serve hot. Serve with hot mustards and sesame seeds.

Vernie Radloff's

MUSTARD DIP

Blend the following in quantities to suit your taste: French's prepared mustard, Colman's dry mustard, brown sugar, horseradish and Worcestershire sauce. Serve with game.

Betty Jeffers'

DUCK SAUCE

Serve with Helen Welty's Roast Duck or any roast game.

½ **Cup currant jelly**
½ **Cup port or sherry**
¼ **Cup catsup**

1 **Teaspoon Worcestershire sauce**
2 **Teaspoons butter**

Combine all ingredients in saucepan and heat.

The
River

MAP TRACES COLUMBIA RIVER BASIN FROM
ORIGIN IN CANADA TO MOUTH AT PACIFIC OCEAN

Seattle Post-Intelligencer Map by Bob McCausland

The River: The Vision and The Reality

As early as 1913 there were people with vision who realized the potential of the Columbia River for public recreation. Attorney R.S. Ludington was one whose 13-year crusade for a civic and recreation center on the River was an uphill battle that came to naught.

Sixty seven years later, during 1980, the first step toward realization of that dream was taken when Chelan Public Utility District (PUD) began implementation of their recreation plan (Exhibit R): property acquisition along the shores of the Rock Island pool.

The $6.7 million recreation plan submitted to the Federal Power Commission for approval in 1967 was a great disappointment to those who had labored for a much more comprehensive plan which had included an interpretive center, an ice arena and boat dock at Sternwheeler Park.

The areas targeted for development: Douglas County Park, Walla Walla Point, Wenatchee River North and South Confluences and the Wenatchee Riverfront, feature principally picnic sites, parking spaces, restrooms, trails, landscaping and boat launching ramps. Improvements at Rock Island have begun.

For 10 years prior to the submission of Exhibit R to the FPC hundreds of people had been involved in an effort to establish specific cultural and recreational concepts in the plan, particularly on the Wenatchee Riverfront. The 1980 beginning represents only the tip of the iceberg. What happens from here is totally dependent on continued community interest and participation.

The following pages sketch briefly principal milestones of community effort during the 1966-1976 period. Space does not permit naming all those who were a part of that effort, but they are remembered in detailed minutes kept of all proceedings; in the meticulous documentation by the Heritage Society of the Mid-Columbia; and the superb and extensive coverage by the Wenatchee World. □

Countdown: The Community and The River

February 1913: "RIVERFRONT PARK NOW OR NEVER" headlines Wenatchee Daily World story. Describes meeting of the Commercial Club, and the appeal of the first riverfront crusader, Attorney R.S. Ludington.

1919: Attorney Ludington reveals 4-block-long riverfront civic and recreational plan, centered at the foot of Orondo Street, designed by Architect Frank Lloyd Wright. This bold and farsighted plan ignored.

March 1926: Attorney Ludington, representing Citizens Parks and Playgrounds Committee, petitions City Commission for $12,000 ($8,000 down) to purchase 30 acres of riverfront land the length of 12 city blocks. Petition rejected. (Current price $35,000 per acre)

1965: National concern for burgeoning, unplanned growth and its consequences surfaces. President Lyndon B. Johnson sponsors WHITE HOUSE CONFERENCE ON NATURAL BEAUTY. Governor Daniel Evans follows with 2 conferences: DESIGN FOR WASHINGTON and DECISIONS FOR PROGRESS.

April 1966: Kirby Billingsley (left) reveals his dream of a Columbia River parkway from the Selkirk Mountains to the sea. Envisions families entering the River at numerous points in small boats, traversing its entire length by portaging around dams or via locks, enjoying historical, cultural, recreational, educational resources at dams, cities, parks along the route. Envisions the River system a mecca for scholars intent on Columbia River's unique culture. Concept later called Stewards of the River.

October 1966: ALLIED ARTS COUNCIL sponsors 2-day conference, DIMENSIONS FOR A GREATER WENATCHEE. Four areas explored: the Arts, Recreation, Urban Planning and Heritage. Heritage and Riverfront Committees emerge. Chairman of the conference: Joan Van Divort, president of Allied Arts Council.

December 1966: Sam Boddy of Allied Arts Council proposes concept for community center on the Riverfront to City Commissioners.

1967-1970: Riverfront Committee embarks on a 3-year program gathering data and involving people in concern on neglected Riverfront. Featured are cleanup campaigns; crusades against industrial encroachment and the proposed Riverfront road; wildlife studies; a probe to determine location of ships burned at the foot of 5th Street; and tours. Plan for changes to Orondo Street Ramp proposed to City Commissioners.

Wilfred Woods, Wenatchee World publisher; Design for Washington Steering Committee; Dimensions I; later Chairman, Community Development Council

Dr. Eva Anderson, sparkplug and chairman, Heritage Committee

Bob Rowe, an organizer of Dimensions conferences 1966 and 1976; author of The Columbia Story for CREST

CREST Studies The River

M.E. Kane, Island View Street resident for nearly 60 years, directed divers Bill Reynolds, Larry Tucker and Russ Carlson as to approximate location of old riverboat remains. A slab of planing containing square nails and two valve wheels, believed from the burned steamers, were recovered.

This was part of the CREST effort to mark the 5th Street pioneer shipyard as a historic place. Inset: CREST president Mike Horan with Larry Tucker.

Riverfront Chairman Ruth Allan with Senator Henry M. Jackson and Congressman Thomas S. Foley prior to DISCOVER OUR RIVER Cruise in 1968.

Design team head Sam Morse; CREST chairman Mike Horan; vice-chairman Joan Van Divort.

1970-1973: Riverfront Committee becomes CREST (Columbia River Environmental Study Team). Design team prepares proposals for land use between Rock Island and Rocky Reach Dams. Campaign begun to build public interest in Riverfront potential, gather endorsements through slide program THE COLUMBIA STORY: Heritage Committee presents weekly programs and studies of Columbia River historical sites, people and events.

1973-1974: Chelan County Regional Planning Council representing City of Wenatchee, Chelan County, Chelan County Port District and outlying communities, appoints 12 to Community Development Council (CDC) to provide specific input to Chelan Public Utility District (PUD) Exhibit R (recreation plan), a Federal Power Commission requirement for licensing construction of the second powerhouse at Rock Island Dam. Council hires Naramore, Bain, Brady & Johanson to prepare Columbia River Master Plan. The project now official and many of its members in CDC, CREST self-destructs.

Dick Bell masterminded CREST Riverfront newspaper survey.

Dr. Paul Larsen, Supt. Tree Fruit Experiment Station; Chairman, Community Development Council (CDC)

Chelan County Commissioners Dave Davis, Fred Nierman, Harry Harn

Bob Parlette, (left) CREST and CDC; and Wenatchee Mayor Jack Grover ponder a problem.

1975: Final draft of Exhibit R endorsed by CDC. Plan includes ice arena, interpretive center and boat dock at Sternwheeler Park in the immediate Wenatchee area. Chelan PUD submits $16 million plan to Federal Power Commission. Puget Sound Power & Light proposes slashing plan to $3 million. Prolonged disagreement as to scope of project ensues.

Sternwheeler Chairman John Jacobson; Planning Director Ed Loidhamer; Public Forums Task Force Nancy Dorsey; Planner Ron Kemp; review recommended alternative to section of Riverfront Master Plan.

March 1976: Allied Arts Council gears up to rally community solidarity behind Chelan PUD $16 million commitment. CITIZENS FOR RIVERFRONT DEVELOPMENT, with Andy Zimmerman, Chairman, organized. HANDWRITING ON THE WALL campaign collects 5,000 signatures for the $16 million plan.

October 1976: DIMENSIONS II, Riverfront Action Conference, re-emphasizes community stand. Promotes Stewards of the River recreational, cultural, scientific, historical concept.

May 1977: Chelan PUD, rejecting scaled-down 11.9 million recreation plan, submits 6.7 million plan to Federal Power Commission.

1980: City of Wenatchee, unable to wait longer for the Center on the Riverfront, completes Wenatchee Center on North Wenatchee Avenue, one of the alternate sites in Riverfront Development Plan.

1980: Chelan PUD begins implementation of Exhibit R through land purchases.

DIMENSIONS II Conference chairman Dr. Ed Hill, later Chairman, Citizens for Riverfront Development.

Jim Wallace, KPQ, produced film "Destination— Wenatchee" for DIMENSIONS II Conference.

A Gathering at the River

Rich Congdon and Nancy and John Jacobson invite friends to their ''Columbia River Park'' — so that they can see how beautiful the River is.

Rich and Nancy

Bob Kintner concentrates on the salmon, while Carl and Peggy Mead chat with Arlene McDonald.

The Confluence

The Wenatchee-Columbia Confluence, home of pioneer Mike Horan family, 1905

During 1971 the Heritage Society of the Mid-Columbia was successful in promoting the Confluence of the Wenatchee and Columbia Rivers as a National Historic Monument.

The North and South Shores of the Confluence are slated for early development in Chelan PUD's Exhibit R (recreation plan).

The Heritage Society proposed a marker for a future roadside park opposite the Confluence near the Columbia River Bridge. Among the many events that transpired at this historic spot are the following:

- Until the 1890s an ancient gathering ground of Pacific Northwest Indians for salmon runs, horse-racing and trading. During the last years Sioux from the Great Plains would join the Central Washington gathering for the Messiah (ghost) dances in a last vain effort to reverse the relentless encroachment by the whites.

- During 1811 David Thompson of Northwest Fur Company passed downriver in a bateau. The same year David Stuart of Pacific Fur Company traded with natives before continuing upriver to establish Fort Okanogan.

- Wenatchee's first business establishment, a trading post, built here during the late 1860s.

- Steamboats at the turn of the 19th century churned up the Columbia carrying passengers and freight for the interior. ☐

Mike Horan - Pioneer at the Confluence

(Report to Heritage Society of the Mid-Columbia by
Kathleen Horan Francies and Pat Horan Wallin.)

The Editor of The Republic prefaced a December 1906 article "Reminiscences of the Olden Times" by Mr. Horan with a statement quoted in part as follows: "Mr. M. Horan is a pioneer of the Wenatchee Valley. He is universally respected, and he, like others, has fought the good fight that those hardy adventurers encountered in the years when the world hereabouts was in its youth. His home on the Wenatchee River is one of the most hospitable—his orchard one of the finest . . ."

When Mike Horan arrived in the Wenatchee Valley in 1889 at the age of 35, he had 23 years of work experience behind him. Orphaned at 12, he and 3 younger sisters struggled for 6 years to stay together. He had worked on freighters, in mines, stone quarries, in the meat business. He had been a San Francisco policeman and had led pack trains into Mount Rainier.

Prior to arrival he had married Margaret Rankin of Cle Elum. When the Horans set up housekeeping they were one of 12 families constituting the population of Wenatchee, which boasted 4 commercial establishments: a general store, a bakery, a blacksmith shop and a saloon. Mike Horan added the fifth: a butcher shop.

The winter of 1889 and 1890 remains the "hard winter" in the memories of those pioneers. Four feet of snow fell in a single night. "The crust on the snow would bear up an ox." Cattle could not exist on the open range and settlers gathered bunches of grass from cliffs and rocks to keep them alive. A milk cow was seen licking paper from a wall to get the paste. Horses were fed pancakes and potatoes. The Columbia River was frozen over, and the Wenatchee River some distance from the mouth.

The settlement ran short of flour. George Blair, with the aid of his "noble beast," Old Sam, broke a road through snow banks 10 to 50 feet deep across the mountains to Ellensburg, where he loaded a half-ton of flour. He arrived back in time to help out the famine. People came in row boats from as far away as the mouth of the Okanogan River for some of the flour.

In 1895 Mike Horan purchased the Sam Miller homestead at the Confluence. Starting with cattle raising he added a dairy business and later planted fruit trees. At one time his pear orchard was the largest in the Valley. For some time he was known as the "Apple King."

During 1901 Mike Horan founded the Washington State Horticultural Association and served as its president until 1914. He inaugurated the orchard practice of allowing weeds to develop and then discing in order to mulch and add humus to the soil. He helped organize Wenatchee city government and served on the council.

The Horans had four living children: John, who married Helen Vandivort; Walt, who married Helen (Sally) Campbell; Esther Horan Bangs and Kathleen Horan Francies.

The huge fruit storage and warehouse complex which now dominates the property bears the wording "Bob McDougall and Sons." The "Sons" are sons of the Mike Horans' granddaughter, Jackie. The gracious white house still stands and in its current role as a restaurant named "The John Horan House," carries on the hospitality for which it was famous in the early days of its glory.

□

The Reincarnated Sternwheeler

During the '70s enthusiasm for the sternwheeler's importance in North Central Washington heritage, and its possibility as an element of the Riverfront cultural plan, sparked formation of the Sternwheeler Committee.

A "workhorse" handling passengers and freight between Wenatchee and the Okanogan and Big Bend country during pioneer days, the reincarnated sternwheeler is visualized as a cultural, recreational, educational and economic element of

*Sternwheeler **Enterprise** in for repairs in the shipyards at the foot of 5th Street.*

the community — a modern "workhorse" on the Rock Island pool.

A focal point for North Central Washington communities, it is seen as a floating workshop, meeting place and performance space for school and community performing arts; a floating facility for meetings, seminars, an adjunct of conventions. For luncheons, parties, dances, receptions. As a museum for sternwheeler memorabilia. A tour boat with banners waving and band playing between Rocky Reach and Rock Island dams during appropriate months of the year.

Columbia River Kitchen

Columbia River Kitchen was created to raise promotional and feasibility study funds and to create interest in the Sternwheeler.

Profits from homemade soups, wholegrain breads, salads and desserts served during the second annual fund-raising effort December 1975 went to the growing Sternwheeler Fund. Chairman of Sternwheeler Committee, John Jacobson. Joan Van Divort headed Columbia River Kitchen.

At right, kitchen workers Karen Jacobson, Rudi Pauly and Mary Joy prepare for event.

STERNWHEELER PARK:
The Old Wenatchee Shipyard

For 21 years — from 1896 to 1917 — Wenatchee was a shipbuilding and repair center for the upper Columbia River. Here at the foot of 5th Street, 15 stern-wheelers were built, beginning with the *Oro* in 1896.

The shipyard property dropped 10 to 15 feet to the Columbia River, then approximately 100 feet east. Building and repairing were done in the drydock area at the northern edge of 5th Street. Here were blacksmith shop with forge and anvil for ironwork; a sail and paint shop; an open lumber and storage building; and a night watchman's house surrounded by fruit trees.

The pumping plant at the southern corner of the foot of 5th Street, though enlarged, is in the same location as it was when the shipyard existed.

On the night of July 8, 1915, the last four ships of the Columbia & Okanogan Steamboat Company: the *Columbia, Okanogan, Chelan* and *North Star,* burned at their moorings.* By the end of the shipbuilding era eight others had been wrecked, burned or had passed out of existence.

To commemorate the shipbuilding era this site was renamed Sternwheeler Park in 1976 and designated a State Historic Place — a project of CREST (Columbia River Environmental Study Team) and the Heritage Society of the Mid-Columbia.

□

Sternwheelers on the Mid-Columbia

Steamboating on the stretch of the Columbia above Rock Island began in July, 1888, when the *City of Ellensburgh* ascended the treacherous Rock Island Rapids under the command of Captain William P. Gray.

For 29 years the steamers were an important North Central Washington transportation link in commerce and travel, handling passengers and freight between Wenatchee and the Okanogan and Big Bend country.

Following the burning of the *Okanogan, North Star, Chelan* and *Columbia* in Wenatchee in 1915, only the *Yakima* and *Bridgeport* carried on the dwindling trade. The *Yakima* was abandoned in 1924 and the *Bridgeport* in 1942, thus ending the era of steamboating, a total of 22 ships over a span of 54 years.   □

*The burning of the ships was a mystery that was solved when an elderly gentleman "confessed" to the late Eva Anderson that he and a friend had been responsible for the fire. As young boys of 8 or 9 they had been swimming in the Columbia (forbidden by their mothers) and had climbed aboard the **North Star** to dry themselves before going home. The little campfire they built was soon out of control, and leaped to the other ships. All their lives they carried their burden of guilt. Only when one of the guilty ones died did the survivor feel free to unburden himself. Their identities are still unknown.*

WENATCHEE-BUILT STERNWHEELERS

Year	Name	Weight(Tons)	Length	Builder	Cost	Disposition	Year
1896	ORO	103	84'	Capt. Finch	$ 1,500	Burned	1898
	Mining steamer. Carried equipment to Okanogan Valley Mines						
1897	ECHO	10	—	Capt. T.H. McMillin	15,000	Wrecked Entiat Rapids	1902
	Shipped via rail from Snohomish River. Carried mail and light merchandise. Crew of 3 men						
1898	CAMANO	59	90'	Capt. T.H. McMillin	—	Wrecked Entiat Rapids	1902
1899	SELKIRK	223	111'	Capt. Griggs	22,000	Wrecked Rock Island Rapids	1906
	Sank while loading wheat at Tramway near Entiat. Salvaged and rebuilt in Wenatchee shipyard						
1899	WENATCHEE (also known as IRISH WORLD) The "hard luck steamer"	77	79'	I.J. Bailey & J.J. O'Connor	—	Burned at foot of Orondo St. while beached for repairs	1901
1900	CHELAN	244	125' 22' beam	C.S. Miller	18,000	Burned at 5th St. shipyard	7/8/ 1915
	Accommodations for 110 passengers. Fastest of Upper Columbia steamers						
1902	GEROME	109	81'	Capt. Griggs	6,000	Wrecked be-tween Pasco & The Dalles	1905
	Sold for use on Lower Columbia						
1902	*NORTH STAR	144	100' 21' beam	Bailey & O'Connor	7,000- 9,000	Burned at 5th St. shipyard	1915
1903	ENTERPRISE	129	85'8''	H.S. Depuy Asst. Will Luke	—	Wrecked at Brewster Ferry	1915
	Wrecked at Entiat Rapids 1906. Salvaged and rebuilt.						
1903	ALEXANDER GRIGGS	—	111'	Believed C&O Steamship Co.	10,000	Wrecked at Entiat Rapids	1905
1905	COLUMBIA	341	150' 25' beam	C&O Steamship Co.	22,000	Burned at 5th St. shipyard	7/8/ 1915
1907	OKANOGAN Largest of the line	432	137' 29' beam	Alexander Watson for C&O S.S. Co.	—	Burned at 5th St. shipyard	7/8/ 1915
1907	*NORTH STAR (Rebuilt)	198	100' 21' beam	Not known	—	Burned at 5th St. shipyard	7/8/ 1915
	Had full-length saloon, ladies' and mens' cabins, dining room, galley, steamheat throughout						
1914	DOUGLAS (first gas-fired)	93	65' 22' beam	Not known		Wrecked at Rock Island Rapids	1920
	Wrecked while enroute to Portland to be sold. Abandoned						
1915	DELRIO	189	80'	Not known	—	Abandoned	1922
1917	NESPELEM (Renamed Robert Young, 1920)	349	154' 26' beam	C.S. Miller	—	Abandoned	1937

From A HISTORY OF THE UPPER COLUMBIA RIVER STERNWHEELERS by Jim Brown and from the archives of Chelan County Public Utility District

STERNWHEELERS NOT BUILT IN WENATCHEE

Year	Name	Weight(Tons)	Length(Feet)	Disposition	Year
1888	CITY OF ELLENSBURGH	213	119	Dismantled	1905
1888	THOMAS L. NIXON	515	159	Dismantled	1901
1901	W.H. PRINGLE	575	166	Wrecked, Entiat Rapids. Repaired. Grounded, Rock Island Rapids	1906
1906	YAKIMA	393	137	Abandoned	1924
1906	ST. PAUL	298	116	Burned, Wenatchee	1915
1917	BRIDGEPORT	438	122	Abandoned	1942

From A HISTORY OF UPPER COLUMBIA STERNWHEELERS by Jim Brown

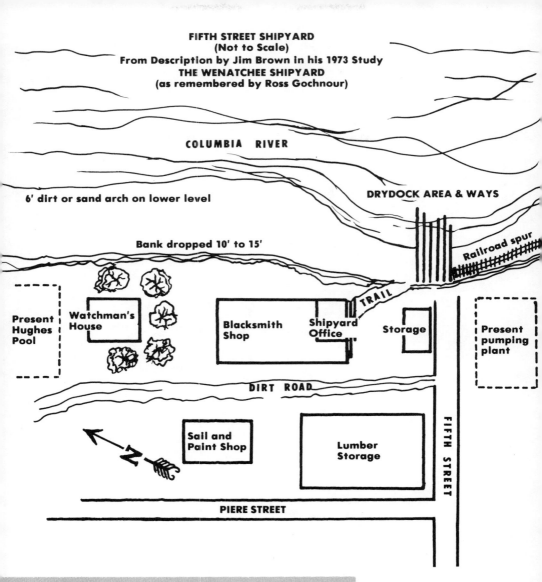

FIFTH STREET SHIPYARD
(Not to Scale)
From Description by Jim Brown in his 1973 Study
THE WENATCHEE SHIPYARD
(as remembered by Ross Gochnour)

COLUMBIA RIVER

6' dirt or sand arch on lower level

DRYDOCK AREA & WAYS

Bank dropped 10' to 15'

Railroad spur

TRAIL

Present Hughes Pool

Watchman's House

Blacksmith Shop

Shipyard Office

Storage

Present pumping plant

DIRT ROAD

N

Sail and Paint Shop

Lumber Storage

FIFTH STREET

PIERE STREET

Steamer being finished at the shipyard in Wenatchee. J. Devereaux said it was great fun to watch when a new steamer was finished and they slipped it into the water.

Dam construction, 1930

Rock Island

A 19-acre site on the west bank of the River directly above Rock Island Dam is slated for development by Chelan PUD. This will consist of a small interpretive center, parking area, picnic sites and dry landscaping.

Rock Island Dam was the first dam built on the Columbia River, completed in 1932. Early explorers found Indians of the Salishan family (they practised flattening of the skull and were also known as ''Flatheads'') who fished at Rock Island. The daughter of Chief Moses, granddaughter of Half Sun, lies buried near here.

Here Chinese miners sluiced a fortune in gold from a west bank ditch abandoned by whites — toiling at night by torchlight, sleeping in riverbank dugouts.

Here in 1888 the ''City of Ellensburgh'' captained by W.P. Grey, became the first steamer to successfully navigate the treacherous Rock Island rapids, later to be known as the graveyard of steamers.

Here in 1893 the Iron Horse crossed the Columbia over the newly-built railroad bridge.

Helen Vandivort Horan told Heritage Society members of the colonization of Rock Island: James Keane, friend of railroad giant J.J. Hill, was believed to be the first white settler to establish home and family, in 1888. Land developers and the railroad attempted to bring settlers in through glowing descriptions of ''wide open spaces, opportunities unlimited — where dollars grew on trees''.

Two companies followed the Siren Song — both arriving in 1909: The Buckeye Colony led by Cap Usher, and the Great Northern Company, led by L.D. Kitchell.

□

THE BUCKEYE COLONY

The E.H. Tryons	The Fay Dots	Mrs. Wallace and son
The Ernest James	The Bert Betsch Family	Mrs. Hattie Martin and
The Tom Brights	The Frank Shause Family	daughter
The Hal Longs	The Harry Spragues	Hugh and Clara Mears
The Frank Giles	Mr. and Mrs. Pike	Dr. Harry & Dr. Madge
The F.R. Gibbons	W.R. and R.W. Voss	Golden
The Joseph Whites	Nellie Tuttle	J.L. Mount
		Herman Conant

THE GREAT NORTHERN COMPANY

The J.C. Melepackers	The Clark Dunkles	The Dan Camerons
The A.A. Vandivorts	The Howard Ellens	The Lon Greers
The William Moores	The Charles Pecks	The LaRues
The H.L. Douglass Family	The William Stones	The Callanders
The Walter Mufflys		

(Right) First Rock Island School: Teacher, Ted Gibbons; Pupils, Kenneth Moore, Pauline Bright and Helen Vandivort

(Below) The bluffs at Crescent Bar, just south of Rock Island Dam

(Right) Indian writings covered by waters behind Rock Island Dam

(Below) A swimming hole at Rock Island. One of a chain of ponds at the base of bluffs north of the town. These ponds encircle the town and at one time were a channel for the Columbia River. They are slated for improvements as wildlife observation areas.

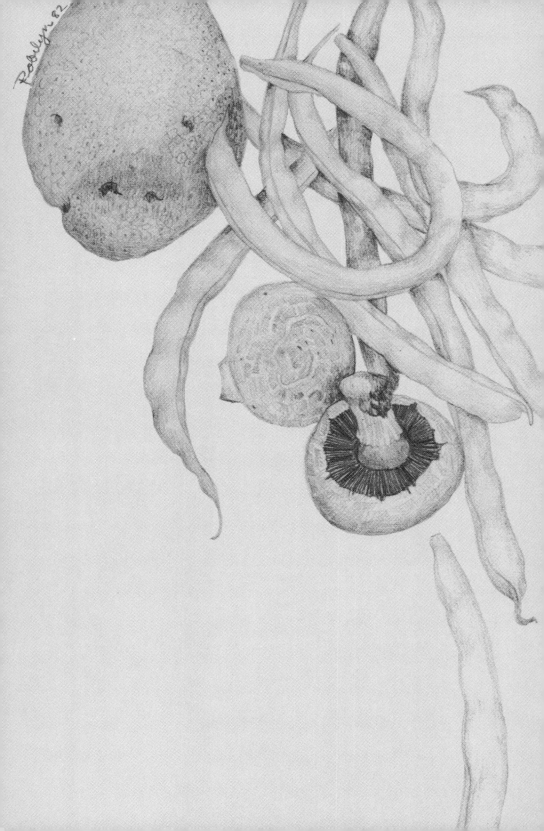

VEGETABLES,
GRAINS, SIDE DISHES

COOKING VEGETABLES

The life-giving vitamins and minerals essential to good health and long life are easily destroyed by the long haul from garden to market to cooking pot; by drowning in cooking water; and by long association with Killer Heat.

The obvious solution is to plant your own little garden patch, or at least toss a few herb seeds among your petunias and tulips. But if that's impossible buy only the freshest vegetables and then get them in and out of the cooking pot as quickly as possible. Two methods of achieving this are through steaming and stir-frying.

STEAMING

If you do not have a steamer, start with as little water in the pot as possible—a half-inch or so. Bring the water to boiling, reduce heat and simmer, covered, until vegetables are tender. The perfect finale is to have a crisp-tender vegetable just as the water disappears. Of course, you could make a steamer by putting a small rack in your cooking pot. Add just enough water so that it will not come in contact with the vegetable.

STIR-FRYING

Stir-frying permits not only retention of nutrients usually lost in cooking water, especially B Vitamins and Vitamin C, but also the chlorophyl responsible for the bright green color of green vegetables. Stir-frying ideally is done in a wok, but a skillet will do. Vegetables are cut in fairly uniform bite-size pieces and cooked over high heat in a little oil, quickly turning and tossing until crisp-tender.

VEGETABLE MEDLEY   2 Servings

Pat Kealoha of Red Rose Cooking School advocated cooking no more than 2 vegetables at a time, both requiring the same amount of cooking time.

2 Tablespoons peanut or
other vegetable oil
½ Cup diced onions
1 Red bell pepper, cut in
½-inch strips
2 Teaspoons water
1 Teaspoon sugar
1 Clove crushed garlic

1 Teaspoon crushed fresh
ginger
1 Cup broccoli flowrets,
cut in 1-inch lengths
1 Cup carrots, cut in
1/8-inch diagonal slices
Salt and pepper to taste

120

Place wok or large skillet over high heat. When pan is hot, add 1 tablespoon of the oil which must be sizzling before you add the bell pepper and onions. Cook, stirring and tossing for one minute. Add ½ teaspoon of sugar and 1 teaspoon water and continue cooking for 1 or 2 minutes longer. (The sugar heightens the green color.) Remove vegetables with slotted spoon and set aside. Add remaining oil to pan. Heat to sizzling. Add crushed ginger and garlic, brown and discard. Add broccoli and carrots; stir-fry for 2 minutes. Add remaining sugar and water, and continue cooking for 1 or 2 minutes longer. Return pepper and onion to pan. Heat. Add salt and pepper to taste. Serve immediately.

CELERY ROOT VINAIGRETTE

Celery root (Celeriac) is a sleeping beauty disguised as an ugly toad. A delicious accompaniment to meat and chicken dishes, especially with an East Asiatic bent.

1 Celery root, cooked until tender in lightly salted water
½ Cup Basic French Dressing (Page 43)

¼ Cup minced parsley
½ Teaspoon sugar
1 Teaspoon celery seeds

Drain cooked celery root and cool. Peel and dice. Toss with remaining ingredients. Chill and serve.

CUCUMBERS WITH SOUR CREAM OR YOGURT

Remember that cucumbers are a "beauty food" when you serve them with baked ham, salmon, chicken or other fowl. Dieters: It's a diuretic, too.

2 Medium cucumbers, peeled and thinly sliced
½ Teaspoon salt
1 Cup sour cream or yogurt
2 Tablespoons apple cider vinegar

1 Tablespoon sugar
2 Tablespoons *each* chopped chives and fresh dill
1 Teaspoon celery seeds (optional)

Sprinkle cucumber with salt and refrigerate for an hour to allow salt to draw out excess moisture. Drain. Combine remaining ingredients and add just before serving. Taste for seasoning. Chill and serve.

"For long life, include in your diet fermented foods such as yogurt, sour milk and sour black bread."

121

CUCUMBER NAMASU

One Hawaiian eveing we enjoyed a Japanese feast at the Pearl City Tavern with Marguerite and Bob Rankin, and Marguerite's sister, Betty Lou. This Japanese restaurant is famous for its Monkey Bar and Bonsai garden. Huge, individual square trays placed before us held bowls of delicious Miso Soup; plates of Beef Sukiyaki; tiny dishes of Sushi, Sashimi, Cucumber Namasu; assorted dips and condiments; and rice.

1 Medium cucumber, peeled and thinly sliced
½ Teaspoon salt, divided
½ Cup rice vinegar
¼ Cup sugar
¼ Cup water
¼ Teaspoon grated fresh ginger
2 Tablespoons grated carrot

Sprinkle cucumber with salt and refrigerate for an hour to draw out excess moisture. Drain. Combine vinegar, sugar, water, ginger, carrot and remaining salt. Mix gently with cucumbers. Chill and serve.

BEET GREENS, MUSTARD GREENS, SWISS CHARD, SPINACH

Dark green means vitamins, iron and minerals.

Wash greens, If young and small, leave whole. If leaves are large, cut in manageable lengths, discarding tough, fibrous parts of stem, particularly in the case of mustard greens. Place in saucepan with only the water already on the leaves. Place on burner, turn heat to high, and when steaming well turn off heat and allow to steam, covered, for 3 or 4 minutes, or until completely wilted. Season with salt and pepper and serve with melted butter, a dash of lemon juice or vinegar; or as is.

GREEN BEANS JULIENNE   Serves 6-8

This isn't the way I usually cook vegetables, but in this particular case the result is so spectacular that I justify the loss of vitamins by saving the bean water for stocks. The green is gorgeous. Try Chinese pea pods cooked this way.

2 Quarts boiling water
3 Tablespoons salt
2 Pounds new green beans, cut julienne
¼ Cup (½ cube) butter, preferably unsalted
Salt and freshly ground pepper to taste

To keep dogs out of your garden, set mousetraps.

122

String the beans if necessary, and trim ends. To julienne, cut in 3 or 4 slivers lengthwise on the diagonal. In a large kettle or saucepan, enameled or otherwise stainless, bring water to rolling boil. Add salt and beans, and boil the beans uncovered over high heat until they are crisp-tender, testing often as they cook. They should be ready in 3 or 4 minutes. The object is to ·preserve maximum flavor, color and vitamins.

Drain the beans in a colander, then dip into a bowl of ice water for 10 seconds to stop the cooking and rinse excess salt. Season with butter, salt and pepper. Turn into serving bowl and serve immediately.

STUFFED MUSHROOMS   Makes 16

This is also a good appetizer.

16 Large mushrooms
 1 Cup finely chopped pecans
   or walnuts
 3 Tablespoons minced parsley
 ¼ Cup melted butter

 1 Clove garlic, minced
 ¼ Teaspoon *each* ground
   thyme ·and salt
   Few grindings of
   black pepper
 ¼ Cup whipping cream

Remove stems from mushrooms. Wipe caps with damp cloth to remove debris, if any. Chop stems and mix with remaining ingredients. Heap into mushroom caps. Arrange in shallow, buttered baking dish. Bake in 350 degree F. oven for 20 minutes, or until stuffing is crisp and lightly brown.

SASTRI'S CHUTNEY   Serves 4

One Christmas holiday a University of Washington engineering student from India was our guest. He prepared the following delicious dish. Although he called it "Chutney", it seems more like a meal in itself to us.

1 Cup *each* cooked green
  beans; cooked rice;
  and cooked, diced
  potatoes with skins
2 Cups buttermilk
½ Cup chopped onions

¼ Cup chopped green pepper
1 Teaspoon lemon juice
½ Teaspoon *each* mustard
  and cumin seeds
¼ Teaspoon turmeric

Place cooked vegetables in serving bowl. Combine remaining ingredients and pour over vegetables. Vegetables may be either hot or cold.

"Confucious refused to eat anything not in season."

PUREED VEGETABLES

Have you noticed how fashionable "pureed" vegetables are these days? My mother served them all the time, only we called them "mashed". A favorite on the farm was a combination of onions, turnips and potatoes, cooked all together and then mashed and served with great globs of home-churned butter, salt and pepper and a sprinkling of minced parsley.

Another favorite was a combination of mashed, cooked carrots and turnips, served as above.

THE SPLENDID POTATO

*One of the memorable events on the Hobart farm was the October harvesting of potatoes, which were sacked and then stored in our root cellar. While the digging was going on my father built a bonfire that gradually burned down and produced a bed of glowing coals. A few of the largest potatoes were buried in the sandy loam beneath the coals, kept glowing and burning with just the right application of firewood. By the time our labors were over, our refreshments were ready. What joy when we dug **these** potatoes, brushed away the ashes, split through the crusty shell, slathered the steaming contents with butter, added a sprinkling of salt and pepper, and then devoured!*

During these times of double-digit inflation it is gratifying to note that potatoes are well worth their nutrition dollar. High in potassium (recommended for heart patients) they provide more thiamine than a dollar spent on any other food. They are second after citrus fruits in Vitamin C, niacin and iron. And if you don't add all the goodies like butter, cream and cheese they are low in calories—only 100 for an average-sized potato weighing 5 ounces. To top it off, they are an antidote for fluid retention and do not drain nutrients from the body in the process!

Ash covered much of Eastern Washington when Mount St. Helens erupted May 18, 1980. At first viewed with alarm and hauled away, the ash began making its way back to southeastern Washington vineyards that had prospered during the initial coverage. In addition to enriching the soil the ash found its way into potters' kilns and emerged as attractive ''Mount St. Helens'' glazes on vases, pots, cups and bowls. —*Photo courtesy U.S. Dept. of the Interior, Geological Survey.*

BAKED POTATOES

Choose the world-renowned Russet Burbank, grown in Idaho and in the Columbia River Basin in soil rich in ash (from perhaps previous Mount St. Helens eruptions) that contributes to its perfection.

Allow one potato per person or one-half if the potatoes are particularly large. Scrub well, snip off a bit of skin at each end to prevent exploding, and place on bottom rack of preheated 400-degree F. oven. Bake for 45 minutes or longer, depending on size of potato. They should be "squeezably soft".

Remove from oven and, using paper towels or cloth, quickly but gently, so as not to break the skin, squeeze and roll each potato, mashing its contents. Split lengthwise down the center, grasp each end and press toward the center, allowing the fluffy contents to erupt. Sprinkle with salt and freshly ground pepper. Serve at once. Eat skin and all.

You may, of course, add a lavish slathering of butter, sour cream or yogurt with bacon bits and snipped chives, minced parsley, fresh dillweed, paprika or whatever seasoning you relish with a baked potato.

BAKED STUFFED POTATOES
Serves 6

6 Large baking potatoes
½ Cup (1 cube) butter, preferably unsalted
1 Cup hot milk or cream, or more if needed

Salt and pepper to taste
¼ Cup chopped chives, parsley or dill
1 Cup shredded sharp cheddar cheese

Preheat oven to 400 degrees F. Scrub potatoes, cut off a bit of skin at each end and bake on bottom rack of oven for 45 minutes, or until soft when squeezed. Slice off top ⅓ lengthwise and scoop pulp into a mixing bowl. Add butter, milk, salt and pepper. Mash with potato masher or whip with electric hand beater until thoroughly smooth and blended. Add herbs and taste for seasoning.

Refill potato shells. Top with shredded cheese. Return to oven and heat for 15 minutes longer. Eat skin and all.

Joyce Stelter's

POTATO ACCORDIANS
Serves 6

6 Medium potatoes, peeled
1 Cup (2 cubes) butter, preferably unsalted, softened

2 Teaspoons Lawry's seasoning salt, or your favorite herb blend

Preheat oven to 375 degrees F. With a sharp knife, make cuts three-fourths down into potato ½-inch apart. In a bowl mix remaining ingredients. Work mixture down into each potato cut. Wrap in foil. Place in baking dish and bake for 30 minutes or longer, until potatoes are tender when pierced.

To bake without foil, place in baking dish and bake, covered, for 30 minutes. Remove lid and continue baking until tender and golden brown.

PLAIN OLD FRIED POTATOES

Serves 4

Men love 'em.

6 Slices bacon, cut
in ½-inch pieces
4 Cups finely sliced peeled
or unpeeled potatoes
½ Cup finely chopped onion

Salt and freshly ground
pepper to taste
Minced parsley for
garnish, if desired

In large frying pan over medium-high heat fry bacon until nearly crisp. Add onion and cook, stirring, for a minute longer. Add potatoes, reduce heat to low and cook, covered for 10 minutes. Add seasonings, turn potatoes, cover and continue cooking for another 10 or 15 minutes, until potatoes are a golden brown and are tender and crisp. Garnish with minced parsley and serve.

DILLED NEW POTATOES WITH PEAS

Serves 4

Chinese pea pods could be substituted for the new peas.

2 Pounds tiny new potatoes,
scraped
¾ Cup water
½ Teaspoon salt

1 Cup new peas
½ Cup heavy cream
2 Tablespoons chopped fresh
dill, parsley or chives

In saucepan over high heat bring ¾ cup water to boiling. Add potatoes and salt. Cover, reduce heat and steam for 15 or 20 minutes, until potatoes are tender. Add peas and steam 3 minutes longer. Drain if necessary. Stir in cream and dill, heat and serve. Melted butter could be substituted for the cream.

POTATOES DAUPHINOISE

Serves 4-6

3 Cups thinly sliced
potatoes
1½ Cups hot milk
1 Egg, beaten
½ Teaspoon salt
¼ Teaspoon white pepper

¼ Teaspoon nutmeg
¾ Cup grated Gruyère or
Parmesan cheese
2 Tablespoons butter,
preferably unsalted
1 Clove garlic

Preheat oven to 350 degress F. Butter a 1½-quart ovenproof casserole and rub with garlic clove.

Quickly whisk beaten egg into the hot milk. Add seasonings and ½ cup of the grated cheese. Mix with sliced potatoes. Transfer to casserole. Sprinkle with remaining grated cheese. Dot with butter. Bake uncovered, until potatoes are tender when pierced.

Dodie Marshall's

POTATOES ROMANOFF

Serves 8-10

This dish may be prepared the day before and refrigerated until ready to bake.

6 Large potatoes
1 Pint sour cream or yogurt
6 Green onions, chopped fine
1½ Cups shredded
   sharp cheddar cheese

Salt and freshly ground
pepper to taste
Paprika

Cook potatoes in their jackets until tender. Preheat oven to 350 degrees F. Butter a 2-quart casserole.

Peel potatoes and shred into a large bowl. Stir in sour cream or yogurt, onion, 1 cup of the cheese, salt and pepper. Transfer to casserole. Top with remaining cheese. Sprinkle with paprika. Bake 20 minutes, or until heated through.

MASHED POTATO CAKES

Form leftover mashed potatoes into cakes and fry in butter until golden brown on both sides. For a richer version add a beaten egg to the potatoes. Minced onion, chives, minced parsley or other favorite herbs are good additions.

Eileen Movius'

CHIVE-BROILED TOMATOES

Serves 8

A beautiful and flavorful complement to any meat, fish or fowl dish.

4 Large, ripe tomatoes
  Salt and freshly-ground
  pepper
½ Cup soft bread crumbs
2 Tablespoons minced chives
  or green onion tops

1 Teaspoon fresh thyme, or
  ½ teaspoon, dried
  Pinch dried sage
¼ Cup (½ cube) butter,
  preferably unsalted
  Grated Parmesan cheese

Preheat oven to 375 degrees F. Remove stem end of tomatoes and cut in half. Salt and pepper cut surfaces. Combine crumbs and herbs, and dip surfaces into mixture. Dot with butter, Sprinkle with Parmesan cheese. Place in baking dish or casserole. Bake 10 minutes, then broil 3 or 4 minutes to lightly brown.

Bonnie Cannon's

TOMATO-ZUCCHINI SAUTE

Bonnie didn't have a name for this dish, but it was a delicious accompaniment to Don's barbecued lobster.

6 Medium tomatoes, peeled
  and quartered
¼ Cup olive oil
2 Medium onions,
  thinly sliced

3 Small zucchini, sliced
½ Teaspoon dried oregano
  or basil
Salt and white pepper
  to taste

In heavy frying pan heat olive oil. Add onions and saute until transparent. Add tomatoes, zucchini and seasonings. Bring to boiling, reduce heat and simmer about 6 minutes, covered, or until zucchini is crisp-tender.

FIRE AND ICE TOMATOES

Tomatoes and cucumbers are simpatico—an unbeatable salad combination. Travelers to Russia and the Balkan countries find them served at every meal.

Try the following fiery combination as an accompaniment to beef, pork or lamb, and watch it disappear.

6 Large, ripe tomatoes,
  skinned and quartered
1 Large green pepper,
  cut in strips

1 Red onion, sliced in
  paper-thin rings
1 Cucumber, peeled and
  thinly sliced

Place prepared vegetables, except cucumber, in a bowl. Pour over them the following sauce:

¾ Cup apple cider vinegar
1½ Teaspoons *each* celery salt
  and mustard seed
½ Teaspoon salt
4 Teaspoons sugar

1/8 Teaspoon *each* cayenne
  and freshly ground
  black pepper
¼ Cup cold water

Place all ingredients in a saucepan over high heat, bring to boiling and boil furiously for one minute. Pour over tomato mixture. Cool. Just before serving add the sliced cucumber.

Zucchini may be substituted for cucumber. Do not peel. Slice and add to the other vegetables *before* the sauce is poured over.

Royal Weinstein's

GLAZED SWEET POTATOES AND APPLES Serves 8

An old family recipe, served as an accompaniment to their Thanksgiving turkey.

8 Spitzenberg or
  Rome Beauty apples
½ Cup sugar
¼ Cup melted butter

2 Cups mashed
  sweet potatoes
Cinnamon

Pour melted butter and sugar into two separate bowls. Pare apples and "crater" them; i.e., core them from the stem end without going completely through to the other end. The "crater" should be about 1½ inches across at the top. Preheat oven to 300 degrees F. Dip apples in melted butter, roll in sugar, fill with sweet potato. Dip again in butter and sugar. Place in baking pan. Sprinkle with cinnamon and put a pat of butter on each. Bake 1½ hours or until tender when pierced, basting frequently until well glazed.

May be prepared the day before and refrigerated up to the point of baking.

BAKED RICE OR WHEAT PILAF Serves 6-8

½ Cup (1 cube) butter,
  preferably unsalted
1 Cup minced onion
2 Cups uncooked brown or
  white long-grain rice,
  washed and drained, or
  2 cups bulgar wheat

4 Cups boiling Chicken Stock
  (Page 16) or
  Beef Stock (Page 23)
1 Teaspoon salt
½ Teaspoon curry powder
  (optional)
Pinch saffron (optional)

Preheat oven to 350 degrees F. In large skillet over medium-high heat saute onions in butter until transparent. Add rice or wheat and cook, stirring for 10 minutes, or until rice is golden (or wheat is golden brown). Add boiling stock, salt and curry powder and saffron, if desired. Cover pan tightly and bake for 30 minutes, or until liquid is absorbed. If rice becomes dry before it is tender, add more stock.

See PILAFF (Page 74).

PLAIN STEAMED RICE 4 Cups

My recipe for plain steamed rice came from an Englishwoman who had spent her youth in Malaya (now Indonesia).

2 Cups uncooked rice,
washed

Water
½ Teaspoon salt

Place rice and salt in top of double boiler. Now this may seem awfully weird, but it works: add enough water to cover rice to the depth of the first joint of your little finger. Cook over simmering water until water is absorbed and rice is tender.

COOKED WILD RICE 4 Servings

1 Cup wild rice
4 Cups Chicken Stock
(Page 16) or equivalent,
canned

2 Tablespoons unsalted butter

Pour rice in a saucepan and cover with cold water. Bring to boiling. Strain. Return rice to pan, add chicken stock, bring to boiling, reduce heat and simmer until all liquid is absorbed, about 30 to 40 minutes. Add butter and serve. Good with game.

RELISHES
& ACCOMPANIMENTS

Robilyn 82

RELISHES & ACCOMPANIMENTS

Janette Bailor's

APPLE BUTTER
6 or 7 Pints

One of the confections available at the Bailors' Earl's Fruit Basket, for several years a roadside mecca for lovers of fruit, honeys and other good things grown in North Central Washington.

10 Pounds sharp apples
  (Jonathan or Winesap)
6 Cups apple cider

2 Cups sugar
4 Drops Oil of Cinnamon

Peel, core and slice apples thinly. Place apples and cider in large kettle and cook until apples are soft. Force through sieve into heavy baking pan. Add sugar and Oil of Cinnamon. Bake in 250 degree oven for 24 hours, stirring every couple of hours.

No, you don't have to stay up all night. Before you turn in, lower heat to 100 degrees and turn up again in the morning. Seal hot in hot, sterilized jars.

BAKED APPLES

How long has it been since you've had a big, squooshy baked apple drowned in thick cream? Quite a while, yes? Rome Beauties are the best. Core as many apples as fit into your baking pan, fill cavities with sugar (brown or white), dot with butter and sprinkle with cinnamon. Pop into 375 degree F. oven and bake until tender when pierced. Scrape up the jellied juices and baste the apples.

Isabella Charbneau Warren's

BAKED PEARS

Cut Bartlett pears in half and remove cores. Fill with brown sugar, dot with butter and sprinkle with cinnamon. Place in baking pan and bake in 350 degree F. oven until tender when pierced.

Pat O'Connor McDaid's

BAKED CURRIED FRUIT
Serves 12

This is one of those recipes that's been around for years and will go on forever. A great accompaniment for sausage, ham and just about any meat dish. Try it with rice dishes. Always a great success for brunch or buffet supper.

2 Cups canned peach halves,
well drained
2 Cups canned pear halves,
well drained

2 Cups canned pineapple
slices, well drained
Maraschino cherries
with stems

Preheat oven to 325 degrees F. In a 1½-quart casserole arrange fruits in layers, with the pineapple slices on top. Place a maraschino cherry in the center of each pineapple ring. Spoon over the fruit the following mixture:

⅓ Cup melted butter
¾ Cup brown sugar

1 Tablespoon curry powder
1 Cup seedless raisins

Bake one hour. May be prepared ahead and refrigerated, in which case reheat 30 minutes at 325 degrees.

Flossie Byrd's
CHILI SAUCE
5 Pints

This versatile relish is wonderful with hamburgers and as an accompaniment to beef dishes, especially pot roast. Mix it with mayonnaise to make Thousand Island Dressing, and with horseradish and catsup for a quick sauce for cracked crab.

4 Cups chopped onions
(about 3 large)
8 Cups tomato pulp and juice
(about 12 tomatoes)
2 Cups chopped sweet green
peppers (about 3 large)
2 Cups chopped sweet red
peppers (about 3 large)

2 Cups apple cider vinegar
1½ Cups brown sugar
2 Teaspoons celery seed
1 Tablespoon salt
2 Tablespoons pickling spice

Blanch tomatoes: immerse in boiling water 1 minute. Remove skin. Wash peppers and remove seeds. Peel onions. Quarter all vegetables. Put through coarse attachment of food grinder. If you use a food processor, be careful not to mince or liquefy vegetables.

Place ground vegetables in a large kettle. Add vinegar, salt, brown sugar and celery seed. Tie pickling spice in a cheesecloth bag and add. Bring to boiling, reduce heat and simmer until thick—about 2 or 3 hours, depending on juiciness of vegetables. Discard cheesecloth bag. Seal in jars.

Al and Carmen's
MUSTARD PICKLES
10 Pints

After years of trial and error my brother and sister-in-law success-fully recalled my mother's wonderful pickles. Serve with Chicken and Dumplings or Chicken Pot Pie.

1 Quart tiny cucumbers, unpeeled	5 Cups cauliflower "flowrets"
1 Quart medium cucumbers, unpeeled, cut in bite-size pieces	2 Cups diced green pepper
	1 Large red pepper, diced
	1 Cup pickling salt (not iodized)
1 Quart tiny pickling onions	

Place vegetables in large, stainless steel or enamel kettle. Pour salt over and cover with water. Cover and soak 24 hours. Drain thoroughly.

6 Tablespoons dry mustard	1 Cup flour
1 Tablespoon turmeric	6 Cups apple cider vinegar
2 Cups sugar	2 Cups water

In 4-quart dutch oven mix the mustard, turmeric, sugar and flour. Add vinegar and water, stirring. Bring to boiling, reduce heat and cook, stirring constantly with a wire whip, until thickened. Be careful not to burn.

Mix with drained vegetables, heat thoroughly and pack in sterilized jars. Seal.

Jackie Gellatly's
PEAR CHUTNEY
3 Pints

Good with poultry dishes. Peaches may be substituted for the pears.

1 Cup white sugar	½ Cup chopped green pepper
1 Cup brown sugar	½ Cup chopped onion
1 Teaspoon ground cardamon	½ Lime, chopped
½ Teaspoon salt	2 Tablespoons chopped fresh ginger or candied ginger
½ Teaspoon dry mustard	
2 Small dried hot peppers, crushed	1 Cup apple cider vinegar
1 Cup raisins	12 Cups chopped Bartlett pears (about 4 pounds)

In dutch oven combine all ingredients except pears. Bring to boiling. Add pears, return to boiling, reduce heat and simmer 45 minutes or until slightly thickened, stirring frequently to prevent sticking and burning. Pour into pint jars. Seal. *Or* freeze in plastic cartons (Jackie says this is preferable).

Janet Gellatly's

SPICED JELLY
10 Glasses

Janet triples this recipe each year for Christmas gifts. Especially good with game.

2½ **Cups water**
  1 **Cup apple cider vinegar**
  4 **Cinnamon sticks**
  2 **Tablespoons whole cloves**
  4 **Teaspoons allspice**

  7 **Cups sugar**
⅓ **1-ounce bottle red**
   food coloring
  1 **Bottle Certo**

Bring to boiling the water, vinegar and spices. Remove from heat and let steep at least 10 minutes, but up to 6 hours. (The longer it steeps the better the flavor). Add sugar. Bring to rolling boil. Add food coloring and Certo and boil hard for ½ minute. Remove from heat. Skim. Pour into jelly glasses and seal with paraffin.

For 47 years—from 1898 to 1945 when it was burned at the direction of Wenatchee Mayor Jack Rogers—''Shacktown'' was home to the otherwise homeless. It sprawled over 60 acres of land lying between the Columbia River and the Great Northern Railway. Fifth Street was its northern boundary.

BREADS,
ROLLS, PANCAKES,
WAFFLES AND ACCOMPANIMENTS

The aroma of baking bread filled the house on Saturdays when a thick slice of hot, buttered bread was something to look forward to.

YEAST BREADS

QUICK BREADS

PANCAKES, WAFFLES AND ACCOMPANIMENTS

YEAST BREADS

WHOLE GRAIN BREAD

The following recipe, developed by the bakers of Columbia River Kitchen, was mixed in large quantities in that blessed invention—the commercial mixer, and beaten about 15 minutes, until the dough left the sides of the bowl. If you have a mixer with a dough hook, by all means use it. The longer this bread is beaten the better its texture. It is full of natural flours and grains, so don't expect it to be feather-light. It is a dense bread.

The original recipe contained gluten, but since it is difficult to find even in health food stores, I have substituted more white flour and more yeast. Experiment and introduce your own grain preferences.

If you have the freezer or refrigerator space, multiply the following by 3 or 4 to save mixing each time you're ready to bake another batch of bread.

8-CUP MIX FOR 2 LOAVES 9 x 5 x 3
½ Cup buckwheat flour
½ Cup rye flour
¼ Cup quick-cooking oats
¾ Cup bran
4 Cups stone-ground whole wheat flour
2 Cups unbleached, all-purpose flour

Place in a small bowl the following ingredients in the order given, and set in a warm place for 15 or 20 minutes, until yeast foams and bubbles up.

2 Cups *very hot* tap water
1 Tablespoon salt
¼ Cup honey
¼ Cup molasses
¼ Cup (½ cube) butter
2 Large eggs, beaten
3 Tablespoons (3 envelopes) dry yeast

To mix in a food processor, follow manufacturer's instructions for mixing bread dough.

If you have a mixer with a dough hook, place dry ingredients and yeast mixture in large bowl. Beat for 5 minutes, until dough leaves sides of bowl. Follow instructions below for rising dough.

To mix manually, place dry ingredients in large bowl. Make a well in the center and pour in the yeast mixture. Stir together until well mixed and formed into a ball. Flours vary, and if it seems too stiff, add warm water. Turn out on lightly floured surface and knead until springy. If it is sticky, add a little more flour. The longer the dough is kneaded the better-textured the bread will be. Place in buttered or oiled bowl, cover with a damp towel and allow to rise in a warm place until doubled in bulk, an hour or more.

Divide dough in 2 equal pieces. On oiled or buttered working surface, flatten each piece and work out bubbles. Form into loaves. Place in buttered or oiled pans. Allow to rise until doubled, about another hour. Bake in preheated 350 degree F. oven for 45 to 50 minutes, or until loaves ring hollow when tapped. Turn out on cooling rack. Brush loaves with butter.

"WHOLE WHEAT" BREAD

For 2 loaves, measure 3½ cups whole wheat flour and 4 cups unbleached all-purpose flour. Follow procedure for Whole Grain Bread. Use 2 tablespoons dry yeast instead of 3.

BASIC WHITE BREAD

For 2 loaves, follow procedure for Whole Grain Bread. Omit molasses. Substitute 7½-8 cups unbleached all-purpose flour for the mixed grains. Use 2 tablespoons dry yeast.

DUTCH CRUNCH TOPPING

Mix 1½ tablespoons sugar, 4 tablespoons dry yeast, ¼ teaspoon salt and ¾ cup rice flour. Add 2 teaspoons vegetable oil and about ⅔ cup warm water. Blend well to form a heavy paste. Cover and let rise in warm place until doubled, about 25 or 30 minutes. Stir down. After shaping loaves and placing in baking pans, spread topping evenly over entire surface. Sufficient for 2 loaves of bread.

SESAME OR POPPY SEED ROLLS   1 to 1½ dozen

Use ½ of Basic Whole Grain, Whole Wheat or White recipe. Following first rising shape into rolls and place in oiled or buttered muffin pans or baking pans. Brush with butter. Sprinkle with poppy or sesame seeds. Allow to rise until doubled. Bake in preheated 350 degree F. oven 15 or 20 minutes, until golden brown.

CINNAMON ROLLS 1 Dozen

Use ½ of Basic Whole Grain, Whole Wheat, or Basic White recipe. After first rising, roll out dough ½-inch thick and 12 inches wide. Spread with ½ cup brown sugar. Sprinkle with 1 tablespoon cinnamon. Roll up and cut into 12 equal pieces. Butter a 9 x 13 baking pan with ¼ cup (½ cube) softened butter. Cover with ½ cup brown sugar and ¼ cup chopped walnuts. Place rolls in prepared pan, cut side up. Allow to rise in warm place until doubled. Bake in preheated 350 degree oven 30 to 35 minutes, until golden brown. Remove from oven, allow to cool 10 minutes and turn out upside-down on foil or other surface prepared to catch dripping syrup.

HAMBURGER BUNS 1 Dozen

Use ½ of Whole Wheat or Basic White Bread recipe. After first rising form dough into 12-inch rope. Cut into 12 equal pieces. Roll and press each piece until a firm ball results. Allow to stand 15 minutes. Flatten each ball to 3 inches in diameter. Place on greased baking sheet 1½ inches apart. Brush with melted butter. Allow to rise in warm place until doubled, about 45 minutes. Bake in preheated 350 degree oven 20 to 25 minutes, or until golden brown.

"FRENCH" BREAD 1 Loaf or 2-3 baguettes

I use PIZZA DOUGH (Page 6). After first rising, knead, then stretch and roll dough, lengthening the loaf and tapering ends. Place diagonally on lightly greased, cornmeal-sprinkled baking sheet. Slash diagonally 5 or 6 times about ¼ inch deep. Allow to rise uncovered 1½ hours, or until doubled in bulk. Bake in 425 degree F. oven for 10 minutes. Reduce heat to 375 and bake 15 minutes longer. Brush loaf with a glaze of 1 egg white fork beaten with 2 tablespoons water. Bake 10 minutes longer, until loaf rings hollow. To form and bake baguettes, see recipe for Caraway Rye Bread.

CARAWAY RYE BREAD 1 Long Loaf, 2 round loaves or 4 baguettes

1½ Cups buttermilk	1 Cup cottage cheese
1 Tablespoon minced onion	2 Tablespoons (2 envelopes)
1 Tablespoon caraway seeds	dry yeast
1 Tablespoon dill seeds	4½ Cups unbleached all-
1 Tablespoon vegetable oil	purpose flour, or
1 Tablespoon salt	more if needed
1 Tablespoon molasses	1½ Cups rye flour

Heat buttermilk in saucepan until very hot. Remove from heat. Add in order given all ingredients except the 2 flours. Allow to stand until yeast bubbles up and foams—about 20 minutes. Combine flours in a large mixing bowl. Make a well in the center and pour in the yeast mixture. Follow instructions for Whole Grain Bread.

When dough has risen, knead and form into loaves. For one long loaf, stretch and roll, lengthening loaf and tapering ends. Place diagonally on greased baking sheet. For 2 round loaves, shape and place in greased 9 inch pie pans. For baguettes, divide dough into 4 equal pieces. Stretch and roll to about 1¼ inches in diameter. Rise on greased baking sheets until doubled. Brush loaves or baguettes with fork-beaten egg white, sprinkle with coarse salt and caraway seeds. Bake in 350 degree F. oven until golden. About 45 minutes for the loaves; 20 minutes for the baguettes, or until they ring hollow when tapped.

GLAZE: One egg white, coarse salt and about 3 tablespoons caraway seeds.

HERBED FRENCH BREAD

1 Loaf French bread	2 Tablespoons minced chives
1 Cup (2 cubes) unsalted	or green onion tops
butter, softened	(or other herbs of
2 Tablespoons minced parsley	your choice)

Blend butter, parsley and chives. You may need more of these ingredients, depending on the size of your loaf and your generosity in slathering the slices. Slice, but do not cut entirely through the bottom crust. Spread mixture on both sides of each slice. Wrap in aluminum foil and refrigerate. *Or* if you are using immediately pop into 425 degree F. oven for 15 or 20 minutes. The slices should be hot.

If you like a garlicky flavor, add minced garlic cloves, as many as you like, to above mixture.

Wendy Jo Pittman's
SOURDOUGH BISCUITS

To honor the Great Northern Railway's legendary Biscuit Man, the town of Leavenworth sponsored an old-fashioned Biscuit Recipe Contest as a Bicentennial event. Grand prize winner Wendy Jo Pittman of Peshastin received an oil painting. Here, in her own words, is her recipe.

2 Cups flour
1 Cup sourdough
1 Cup warm water
1 Tablespoon molasses

1 Tablespoon honey
2 Tablespoons bacon fat
1 Teaspoon salt
Sprinkle wheat germ

Melt bacon fat and cool. Mix flours together—whole wheat, rye, or whatever, in a bowl. Dig a hole in the center and pour in sourdough. Mix in gradually with warm water, leaving enough dry flour around bowl to form manageable dough.

Let sit in warm place ½ hour to 1½ hours. Add molasses, honey, salt, bacon fat and wheat germ. Add just about anything you're in the mood for—a touch of buttermilk for flavor, caraway seeds or whatever.

Mix all together in the center and kinda pat all the extra flour around the sides to make a good, firm dough. Temperature will have to vary. I cook on a Round Oak Chief wood cook stove and I cook 'em at 375 degrees to 400 for 20 to 30 minutes.

Anyway, gather your dough up into little balls. Grease an iron skillet—get it hot—put your little round balls in the skillet making a circular design with one in the middle. Let that rise up on top of your stove (If you have a wood stove—if not, in a warm place), for half an hour or until double. Then bake. They are the best biscuits.

Alma Johnson's

COFFEE BREAD (Swedish Cardamon Bread)   2 Loaves

A neighbor when we lived on the Hobart farm, Alma baked wonderful Swedish things.

2 Cups milk, scalded
1 Cup sugar
½ Teaspoon salt
¼ Cup butter,
   preferably unsalted
2 Large eggs
1 Egg yolk

2 Tablespoons (2 envelopes)
   dry yeast
7 Cups unbleached,
   all-purpose flour
1 Teaspoon cardamom

Heat milk until film forms on top. Pour into medium bowl. Add next six ingredients in the order given. Allow to stand until yeast foams and bubbles up.

In a large bowl place the flour and cardamom. Make a well in the center and pour in the yeast mixture. Stir until well mixed. Continue to stir and beat vigorously until dough leaves the sides of the bowl and forms a ball, about 5 minutes. Place in a buttered bowl, cover with a damp towel and allow to rise in a warm place until doubled in bulk, an hour or so.

Divide in 2 equal pieces. On lightly floured working surface knead for a minute or 2 and form into loaves. Place in buttered pans. Allow to rise until doubled. Brush lightly with Egg White Glaze. Bake in preheated 350 degree F. oven until loaves ring hollow when tapped. Remove to wire racks to cool.

EGG WHITE GLAZE: Beat together with a fork until well mixed 1 egg white with 2 tablespoons sugar.

CHRISTMAS BREAD

Follow Alma Johnson's Coffee Bread recipe. Work in ½ cup mixed glacéed fruits and 1 cup seedless raisins after flour is added.

CHRISTMAS RING   2 Rings

Follow Alma Johnson's Coffee Bread recipe. Divide dough in half. Roll out into a rectangle about 18 x 10 inches. Spread with ½ cup softened butter. Sprinkle with ½ cup brown sugar, ½ cup chopped walnuts, ½ cup raisins, ½ cup chopped candied cherries or mixed glacéed fruits. Roll up firmly beginning from the long side. Transfer dough to greased baking sheet. Bring the two ends together to form a circle. Moisten ends with water to seal, concealing seam as neatly as possible.

With scissors cut from outside of ring ¾ of the way into the center, making an even number of cuts at about 1 or 1½-inch intervals. Twist each slice over on its side to reveal the contents. Roll out other half of dough and repeat procedure.

Cover and allow to rise in warm place until doubled in bulk, about 45 minutes. Brush lightly with Egg White Glaze. Bake in preheated 350 degree F. oven about 35 to 40 minutes, or until golden brown. Remove to wire racks to cool.

Frost with a glaze of ½ cup powdered sugar and 1 tablespoon water. Decorate with candied cherries and "leaves" cut of citron.

QUICK BREADS

BAKING POWDER BISCUITS About 1 dozen

2 Cups unbleached
    all-purpose flour
3 Teaspoons baking powder
½ Teaspoon salt

½ Cup (1 cube) butter,
    preferably unsalted
¾ Cup milk

Sift together the dry ingredients. Work in butter with your fingers, rubbing until the consistency of cornmeal. Add milk to make a soft dough. Turn out on a floured surface and knead for a minute or so. Roll out to ¾-inch thickness and cut into rounds with a 1½-inch or 2-inch cookie cutter.

Arrange on lightly greased baking sheet: close together if you want them fluffy around the edge—farther apart if you want them crisp all around. Bake in 450 degree F. oven for 15 minutes, or until tops are golden brown.

Serve immediately with butter and jelly or jam.

BLUEBERRY MUFFINS 1 Dozen

Currants raisins or cranberries could be substituted, but who can resist a blueberry muffin?

2 Cups unbleached,
    all-purpose flour
2 Tablespoons sugar
2 Teaspoons baking powder
½ Teaspoon soda
¼ Teaspoon salt
2 Large eggs

1 Cup buttermilk or yogurt
¼ Cup (1 cube) melted butter,
    preferably unsalted
1 Cup blueberries
1 Teaspoon grated orange
    rind
    Sour Cream Brunch
    Cake Topping (Page 174)

Preheat oven to 375 degrees F. Grease well 12 large muffin cups. In a medium bowl sift together the dry ingredients. In another bowl beat together the eggs, buttermilk and melted butter. Pour egg mixture into dry ingredients and just barely mix to moisten flour. Add blueberries and orange rind. Spoon batter into muffin cups. Sprinkle with Topping and bake for 25 minutes, or until a toothpick inserted in center comes out clean. Let rest for 5 minutes. Run knife around muffins to loosen and remove carefully. (Sometimes the blueberries sink to the bottom and want to stay down there in the pan).

NEW ENGLAND CORN BREAD

And what, pray tell, is better with baked beans?

1 Cup yellow cornmeal
1 Cup *sifted,* unbleached,
  all-purpose flour
4 Teaspoons baking powder
2 Tablespoons sugar
  (optional)

½ Teaspoon salt
1 Large egg, beaten
1½ Cups milk
¼ Cup (½ cube) melted butter,
  preferably unsalted

Preheat oven to 400 degrees F. Grease well an 8 x 8 baking pan. In a medium bowl combine dry ingredients. Add egg to milk and mix with dry ingredients. Add melted butter, and mix thoroughly. Pour into baking pan. Bake for 25 minutes, or until cake tester or toothpick inserted in center comes out clean. Serve hot, cut in squares.

POPOVERS   1 Dozen

*I couldn't believe it, but yes—it's true. These **are** foolproof. Delicious hot, slathered with butter and a dab of jam along with your omelet.*

1 Cup milk
1 Cup flour

2 Large eggs
¼ Teaspoon salt

Butter well 12 muffin cups. Place in a bowl all ingredients and with a spoon *just barely mix.* Dry ingredients need only be moistened. Disregard the lumps.

Pour muffin cups half full. Place in cold oven. Set oven at 450 degrees F. Set timer for 30 minutes and forget it. When timer buzzes, open the oven door and take out your popovers. What a lovely surprise!

Anna Vandivort's
BANANA BREAD   1 Loaf

My mother-in-law's Banana Bread recipe is the best, in my humble opinion.

½ Cup (1 cube) butter,
  preferably unsalted
1 Cup sugar
2 Large eggs, beaten
2 Cups unbleached,
  all-purpose flour

½ Teaspoon salt
1 Teaspoon soda
3 Bananas, mashed
  Raisins and/or nuts
  (optional)

147

Butter a 9 x 5 x 3 loaf pan. Preheat oven to 350 degrees F. Cream butter and sugar. Add eggs. Sift together and add dry ingredients. Blend thoroughly. Add mashed bananas. Add raisins and/or nuts, if desired. Pour into prepared pan. Bake 45 to 50 minutes, or until cake tester or toothpick inserted in center comes out clean. Turn out on rack to cool.

Elaine Monroe's

ZUCCHINI HEALTH BREAD 4 Loaves

I found that for my personal taste 2 cups of sugar were more than ample for this large recipe.

6 Eggs	4 Cups all-purpose flour
4 Cups sugar	1 Cup whole wheat flour
2 Cups vegetable oil	1 Cup wheat germ
4 Teaspoons vanilla	4 Teaspoons soda
4 Cups shredded, unpeeled	1 Teaspoon baking powder
zucchini, packed	1 Tablespoon cinnamon
2 Cups crushed pineapple	1½ Teaspoons nutmeg
2 Teaspoons salt	2 cups finely chopped nuts
	2 Cups currants or raisins

Grease four 9 x 5 x 3 loaf pans. Preheat oven to 350 degrees F. Beat together eggs, sugar, oil and vanilla until thick and foamy. With a spoon stir in zucchini and pineapple. Combine next 8 ingredients and stir into zucchini mixture. Add nuts and currants. Bake for 1 hour, or until toothpick or cake tester in center comes out clean.

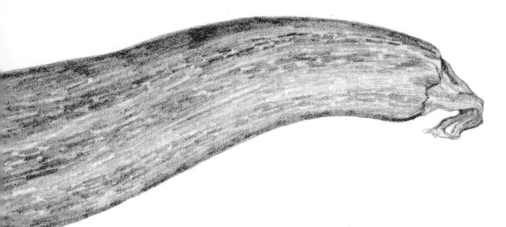

PANCAKES, WAFFLES & ACCOMPANIMENTS

BUCKWHEAT PANCAKES
Serves 4

The all-time favorite when the family gathers at the Lake Wenatchee cabin and the wood-burning stove goes into action. Always baked on the iron "spider" brought from Pittsburgh when the Vandivort family came to Wenatchee.

2 Eggs, beaten	1 Cup unbleached,
1½ Cups milk	all-purpose flour
½ Cup melted butter	½ Teaspoon salt
1 Cup buckwheat flour	2 Teaspoons baking powder

Add milk and melted butter to beaten eggs. Sift together dry ingredients and add. Batter should be quite thin. Add more milk if necesssary. Drop by spoonfuls on hot griddle over medium-high heat, spreading thinly. Turn when bubbles appear, and cook until browned.

Buttermilk may be substituted for the sweet milk, in which case add ½ teaspoon baking soda and decrease baking powder to 1 teaspoon.

TOPPINGS: Serve with wild blackberry, blackcap or huckleberry jam. Or canned wild berries with whipped cream, or crushed fresh, sugared strawberries, or freshly made applesauce, or fried apple slices.

FRIED APPLE SLICES
Core Golden Delicious apples. Do not peel. Cut in thick slices. Cook gently in frying pan in butter, turning carefully. Sprinkle with sugar and cinnamon.

CHEESE BLINTZES
Makes 16

An enduring memory of San Francisco: The Vienna House and the luscious cheese blintzes topped with fresh strawberries and whipped cream.

This was a much-in-demand Columbia River Kitchen dessert. Serve for Sunday breakfast with crisp bacon.

1 Recipe Basic Crêpe Batter (Page 66)	Filling and Toppings

Bake crêpes about 6 inches in diameter. Place a tablespoonful filling on each crêpe. Fold into envelope shapes or roll up into cylinders. (At this point they may be wrapped in foil or plastic wrap and stored in the freezer until ready to serve).

Fry both sides quickly in butter over medium-high heat until golden brown. Spoon over desired topping. Serve immediately.

FILLING

1 Pint cottage cheese	2 Teaspoons grated lemon
2 Egg yolks	rind, or 1 teaspoon vanilla
1 Tablespoon soft butter,	2 Tablespoons sugar
preferably unsalted	

Place all ingredients in food processor or mixer and blend thoroughly.

TOPPINGS: Sour cream; crushed strawberries; berry or apricot jam or jellies; powdered sugar and cinnamon.

DUTCH BABIES   Serves 4

Bring drama to the table! This is a fantastic breakfast, brunch or supper dish. The following will serve 4. Be on the safe side and have 2 pans ready to go. Mix a second batch while the first is baking. Bake in a skillet, paella pan or other ovenproof baking dish or pan large enough to hold 4 quarts, and not more than 3 inches deep.

¼ Cup (½ cube) butter,	1 Cup milk
preferably unsalted	1 Cup unbleached
4 Large eggs	all-purpose flour

Preheat oven to 425 degrees F. Place butter in pan and set in oven. While butter is melting quickly mix batter. Place eggs in blender and set at high speed for one minute. Gradually add milk and slowly add flour. Continue blending for 30 seconds longer. (If you are mixing by hand, beat eggs until thick and lemon-colored. Add milk and flour gradually.)

Remove pan from oven and pour in the batter. Bake until puffed and lightly browned—about 20 or 25 minutes. Bring to the table immediately. Cut in wedges and serve. It will fall while you're doing it, but don't let that worry you.

TOPPINGS

Honey, fruit syrups, maple syrup. Powdered sugar and lemon. Wild berry, apricot, raspberry, strawberry jams. Crushed fresh strawberries, fresh peach slices. Fried Golden Delicious apple slices with cinnamon, powdered sugar and a squeeze of lemon.

"Everyone has some character experience that tests his or her quality".

Willa Parks'
FRENCH HOTCAKES
Serves 4

*Formerly with **Alcoa** in Wenatchee, the Parks live in Pittsburgh. Willa's delectable pancakes came to me through Joyce Stelter.*

4 Eggs, separated
1 Cup milk
½ Teaspoon salt
2 Teaspoons sugar

1 Tablespoon melted butter
⅔ Cup unbleached,
   all-purpose flour
¼ Teaspoon baking powder

Beat egg whites until stiff. Set aside. Beat egg yolks until thick and lemon-colored. Add milk, salt, sugar and melted butter. Sift together flour and baking powder and add. Fold in gently the beaten egg whites. Drop by spoonfuls on hot buttered griddle over medium-high heat. Turn when bubbles appear, and cook until browned.

Serve with melted butter, jam and powdered sugar. Roll up if desired.

GRATED APPLE PANCAKES
Use preceding recipe. Pour thin layer of batter on griddle and spread. Place spoonful of grated apple in center and spread toward edges. Cover apple with a little batter. When bubbles appear, turn and brown.

PIONEER PANCAKES

Chef Michael Farano told Heritage Society of the Mid-Columbia members of the diets of wagon train pioneers and of the difficult conditions under which women prepared the meals.

Breakfast and supper, as long as supplies held out, might be the same: fried ham, panbread, tea or coffee, or a brew made of scorched seeds or dried fruit. No fresh fruits or vegetables. Water for drinking and cooking might be muddy or full of mosquito larvae. Meals were cooked over wood, sagebrush or dried manure open fires in all kinds of weather.

2 Tablespoons porcupine fat
1 Pound flour
1 Teaspoon salt
½ Pint water

1 Goose or seagull egg
1 Heaping teaspoon
   baking soda

Mix and put into skillet. Bake until it bubbles. Flip and cook the other side.

POTATO PANCAKES
Serves 4

This hearty pancake is from my mother's repertoire. Serve with ham, bacon or sausage, eggs and applesauce for a complete meal. Good with jellies or jams.

2 Cups peeled, grated
  raw potatoes
½ Teaspoon salt

1 Teaspoon sugar
2 Tablespoons flour
2 Eggs, beaten

Sprinkle salt over potatoes and allow to stand 15 minutes. Squeeze out moisture and add remaining ingredients. Bake on lightly greased griddle over medium heat, spreading batter thinly. Brown on both sides.

CRÊPES AU FROMAGE
17 7-inch Crêpes

Adapted from The London Cordon Bleu Cookery School version, given in San Francisco, where I attended a 4-day session. A great accompaniment to roast meat.

1 Recipe Basic Crêpe
  Batter (Page 66)
½ Cup grated sharp cheddar
  or Gruyère cheese

Béchamel Sauce
Topping

Add cheese to basic crêpe batter. Blend. Let batter stand at least 30 minutes, preferably overnight. Bake crepes on lightly greased, heated griddle. Spread a generous tablespoon of Béchamel Sauce on each crêpe, and roll up like cigars. Place in buttered ovenproof dish, leaving separation so that they will crisp. Sprinkle with grated cheese, dot with butter and bake at 400 degrees F. for 7-10 minutes, or until lightly brown. Sprinkle with minced parsley and serve very hot.

BÉCHAMEL SAUCE

¼ Cup flour
¼ Cup (½ cube) butter
2 Cups scalded milk (infused
  with a slice of onion,
  5 peppercorns, dash of
  mace, and a bay leaf)

Salt and white pepper
to taste

Melt butter in saucepan over medium-high heat. Add flour, lower heat and cook, stirring and blending for 3 or 4 minutes. Strain milk and add all at once, stirring briskly until thickened. Remove from heat. Keep warm.

TOPPING

½ Cup grated cheese (half
  Parmesan and half
  Gruyère or sharp cheddar)

1½ Tablespoons butter
1 Tablespoon minced parsley

BELGIAN WAFFLES
Makes 3-8 inches square

*Waffles have been popular in Western Europe for more than 800
years. The Dutch gave them their name, meaning "honeycomb". Serve
these with sliced strawberries and whipped cream.*

1¼ Cups unbleached,
  all-purpose flour
1 Cup water
2 Tablespoons sugar
2 Teaspoons baking powder

2 Teaspoons vanilla
½ Teaspoon cinnamon
½ Teaspoon lemon extract
1 Cup whipping cream,
  beaten stiff

Beat together flour and water until smooth. Stir in sugar, baking
powder, vanilla, cinnamon and lemon extract. Fold in whipped cream.
Let stand 15 minutes. Spoon batter in heated, seasoned Belgian waffle iron, or electric waffle iron brushed with melted butter. Bake according to manufacturer's directions.

SUNDAY WAFFLES
Serves 4

*The grandchildren's favorite breakfast. Serve with toppings suggested
for Buckwheat Pancakes and Dutch Babies.*

2 Large eggs, beaten
  until light
2 Cups milk
6 Tablespoons melted butter,
  preferably unsalted
2 Cups unbleached,
  all-purpose flour

¼ Cup cornmeal
2 Teaspoons baking powder
½ Teaspoon salt

Add milk and melted butter to eggs. Sift together dry ingredients and
add. Spoon batter in seasoned waffle iron and bake according to
manufacturer's directions.

WHOLE GRAIN WAFFLES: Substitute 1 cup whole wheat, buckwheat or other whole grain flour for 1 cup white flour.

DESSERTS

COOKIES

CAKES, FILLINGS AND FROSTINGS

If there's anything that's worth the effort it's a home-baked cake with the old-time, satisfying richness and goodness that can come only when the best ingredients are used. Arrange the baking so the aromas hit the troops as they come in the door.

Rosilyn

PIES AND PIE CRUSTS

CORDIALS, WINES AND CONFECTIONS

DESSERTS

APPLE BETTY   Serves 6-8

Another medium for Columbia River Country apples and your over-the-hill bread. Serve hot or cold, with cream if desired.

**5 Cups peeled, diced or
   sliced Jonathan, Yellow
   Transparent, Staymen,
   Spitzenberg, or
   Gravenstein apples
2½ Cups crumbled bread
 ½ Cup (1 cube) butter,
   preferably unsalted**

**¾ Cup brown sugar, packed
1 Teaspoon cinnamon
½ Teaspoon nutmeg
½ Teaspoon grated lemon peel
¼ Teaspoon salt
½ Cup water**

Preheat oven to 350 degrees F. Butter a 2-quart baking dish. Place layer of apples in bottom of baking dish. Sprinkle with a layer of bread, sugar, cinnamon, nutmeg and lemon peel. Dot with butter. Repeat until dish is full, ending with bread on top. Add salt to water and pour into dish. Bake uncovered 45 minutes to an hour, or until apples are tender and pudding is nicely browned.

APPLE DUMPLINGS   Serves 6

Apple Dumplings are as American as apple pie. Serve this old-fashioned dessert either hot or cold with thick cream. Or just as is with the lovely, syrupy juices spooned over.

**½ Recipe Basic Pie Crust
   (Page 181) or 1 Recipe
   Shortcake Dough
   (Page 177)
6 Medium Rome Beauty
   apples, peeled and cored
1 Cup brown sugar**

**6 Tablespoons butter,
   preferably unsalted
Cinnamon
Grated lemon peel
Egg, fork beaten,
   for pastry glaze**

Preheat oven to 425 degrees F. Roll out pastry to 1/8" thickness. Cut into 6 to 8-inch squares, depending on size of apples. Place apple in the middle of each square. Fill center with sugar. Sprinkle with cinnamon, dot with butter and grate lemon peel over. Bring corners up to top of apple, bring edges together, moistening edges with water if necessary to seal and cover apple completely. If desired, scraps may be cut into decorative leaves to cover tops. Place dumplings in baking pan about an inch apart. Brush with egg glaze and bake 15 minutes. Reduce heat to 350 degrees and bake 30 to 40 minutes longer, or until apples are tender when pierced, and pastry is golden brown.

CHOCOLATE BAVARIAN

One of Columbia River Kitchen's most popular desserts. Here's the perfect place for some of your own breadcrumbs, recycled from bread ends, leftover waffles, dried-out rolls, etc. Demolish with a rolling pin, blender or food processor. Taste them, and if not sweet enough, add a little sugar.

2 Cups dry breadcrumbs or vanilla wafer crumbs	¼ Cup Kahlua (Page 192)
½ Cup (1 cube) melted butter, preferably unsalted	5 Large eggs, room temperature, separated
½ Teaspoon ginger	¼ Teaspoon salt
¼ Cup orange juice	2 Teaspoons vanilla
1 Tablespoon (1 envelope) unflavored gelatin	2 Cups whipping cream
1⅓ Cups chocolate chips	¼ Cup powdered sugar
	1 Cup chopped walnuts or pecans

Make crust ahead. Mix thoroughly the crumbs, melted butter and ginger. Press firmly to bottom and sides of 9-inch springform pan. Refrigerate.

Sprinkle gelatin over orange juice to soften. Place chocolate chips and Kahlua in pan over simmering water. When chips begin to melt remove from heat, stirring occasionally until completely melted. Add softened gelatin. Stir until dissolved. Cool.

Beat egg yolks until thick and lemon-colored. Blend in salt, 1 teaspoon of the vanilla and the chocolate mixture. Whip until stiff 1 cup of the cream and fold in gently. Beat egg whites until stiff and fold into chocolate mixture. Pour into crumb-lined pan. Refrigerate until firm.

When ready to serve, remove rim. Ease onto serving plate. Beat remaining cup of cream with powdered sugar and remaining vanilla. Pile on top of Bavarian. Sprinkle with chopped nuts. Serve thin slices.

RENAISSANCE OF THE OLD-FASHIONED PUDDING

Baked Custard, Rice, Bread and Fruit Puddings were prepared often by my mother, especially during periods of convalescence. Their old-fashioned wholesomeness is at home in today's atmosphere of growing nutrition and pocketbook consciousness, as evidenced by their popularity in all the gourmet magazines!

157

BAKED CUSTARD
Serves 6

3 Cups milk	1 Teaspoon vanilla
4 Large eggs	¼ Teaspoon salt
¼ Cup sugar	Cinnamon or nutmeg

Preheat oven to 325 degrees F. Butter a 1½-quart casserole or 6 custard cups. In the top of a double boiler over simmering water scald the milk. In a bowl beat lightly together the eggs, sugar, salt and vanilla. Add scalded milk, stirring constantly while adding. Pour into baking dish. Sprinkle with cinnamon or nutmeg. Place in a pan of hot water at least 1 inch deep.

Bake 45 minutes to an hour for the casserole, or 20 to 25 minutes for the custard cups or until set and a silver knife inserted in the center comes out clean. *Do not permit the water to boil or your custard will curdle.* Add cold water a time or two during baking to prevent it. Remove from oven, cool and serve.

FRESH PLUM PUDDING
Serves 6-8

The following recipe may be used with any fresh fruit: peaches, apricots, prunes. My mother made it with berry and fruit juices. Delicious chilled and served with real cream.

4 Cups plum puree	Pinch of salt
Sugar to taste	½ Cup cornstarch

To make puree, place plums in pan with just enough water to barely cover. Bring to boiling, reduce heat and simmer gently until soft. Force through sieve or food mill.

Mix sugar, salt and cornstarch with ½ cup of the plum puree. In saucepan pour the rest of the pulp, bring to boiling over high heat, stirring to prevent burning. Add cornstarch mixture, stirring. Reduce heat and cook until thickened. Remove from heat, cool and pour into serving bowl.

INDIAN PUDDING

During the Bicentennial I followed with a great deal of interest the Great Indian Pudding Controversy in Craig Claiborne's column in the Seattle P-I, and concluded that the following from Mrs. Rufus Woods' collection is as authentic as any.

158

"Scald one quart of milk, when boiling hot stir in three tablespoons of corn meal, the same of flour, wet up with cold milk and one tablespoon of butter. Let cool and add a well-beaten egg, one-half cup of sugar, one-quarter cup of molasses, one-half teaspoon of ginger, one-half teaspoon of cinnamon. Add one-quarter pint of cold milk and bake three hours. Eat with hard sauce".

RICE CUSTARD PUDDING   Serves 6-8

Sometime when you're cooking rice as an accompaniment to a main dish or soup, cook a little extra and make this delicious pudding.

2 Cups cooked rice	¼ Cup honey or sugar
½-1 Cup raisins (optional)	¼ Teaspoon salt
3 Cups milk	1 Teaspoon vanilla
4 Large eggs, beaten	Nutmeg or cinnamon

Preheat oven to 350 degrees F. Butter a 2-quart baking dish or casserole. Mix rice and raisins and spoon into casserole. Blend milk, eggs, honey or sugar, salt and vanilla. Pour over rice and raisins and mix gently with a fork. Sprinkle with nutmeg or cinnamon. Set in a pan of hot water at least one inch deep. Bake 45 minutes or longer, until silver knife inserted in center comes out clean. *Do not permit water to boil or custard will curdle.* Add cold water a time or two to prevent it. Serve hot or cold, with cream if desired.

BREAD PUDDING

We ate a lot of this on the farm!

Follow recipe for Rice Custard Pudding. Substitute 4 cups stale broken bread for the rice.

ENTERTAINMENTS

In the days before our radio and piano, music came from a Sears Roebuck phonograph. My father's favorite Wagner "Overture to Die Walkure" often awakened us in the early morning hours. Young people came to our house with the latest records. The girls shimmied to "Blues My Naughty Sweetie Gave to Me", beautiful with their hair in puffs and their georgette blouses.

According to James Beard you can be old, fat and ugly, but if you are a good cook the world will beat a path to your door.

159

There were square dances in our barn, and I remember the stomping and breathless laughter and lively fiddling. All-night occasions were these—when children fought sleep in the hayloft, stretching their necks over the edge for a peek at the dancers below—and the long table against the wall, glorious in its drapery of white and its burden of home-smoked hams and sausages, fried chicken, potato and fruit salads, sandwiches of home-baked breads, gelatin puddings, pies, cakes, cookies and lemonade.

Kerosene lanterns hung at intervals around the dance floor, casting a pale yellow glow on the convivial scene.

There were Saturday night theatricals organized by Mrs. Arthur Brown. I remember one in our living room when Mrs. Oscar Johnson and my father sang "Blue Bell", and my mother, with her hair down, sang "Let the Rest of the World Go By".

Afterwards, my mother served Cream Puffs, and when Mr. Brown picked his up and impetuously bit into it, the whipped cream squirted all over his mustache and down the front of his vest.

Katherine's

CREAM PUFFS

A French classic—easy to make.

PÂTE À CHOUX

1 Cup water
½ Cup (1 cube) butter, preferably unsalted
1 Cup unbleached all-purpose flour

½ Teaspoon salt
4 Large eggs

Preheat oven to 450 degrees F. Lightly butter a baking sheet.

Pour water in medium saucepan, bring to boiling, add butter and bring again to a rolling boil. Add flour and salt all at once, stirring vigorously with a wooden spoon. As soon as mixture leaves sides of pan and forms a ball (a minute or so) remove from heat. Cool slightly. Add eggs, unbeaten, one at a time, beating after each addition until smooth.

Using a wet tablespoon, drop by spoonfuls on baking sheet about 2 inches apart. Place in center of oven and bake for 10 minutes. Reduce heat to 300 degrees. Bake 30 minutes longer. Puffs should be high and golden in color. Remove from oven. Cool. Split in half. Scoop in filling. Sprinkle with powdered sugar.

FILLING

2 Cups whipping cream	1 Teaspoon vanilla
¼ Cup powdered sugar, plus extra for garnish	

Beat whipping cream, powdered sugar and vanilla until stiff.

CHOCOLATE ECLAIRS

Prepare Pâte à Choux. Drop by spoonfuls on lightly buttered baking sheet. Elongate 3 to 5 inches, or the length you desire, or use pastry bag. Follow baking directions for Cream Puffs. Cool, split, fill and frost.

FILLING: Prepare CHIFFON PIE FILLING (Page 182) or whipped cream filling (above).

GLAZE

1 6-ounce package chocolate chips	1 Teaspoon vanilla
	1 Cup sour cream

Melt chocolate chips over hot water. Add vanilla. Stir in sour cream.

ICE CREAM DESSERTS

Delicious desserts can be made in seconds by pouring non-alcoholic syrups or a shot of liqueur such as Triple Sec, Grand Marnier, Cherry Heering, Curacao, Crème de Menthe, Kahlua, Benedictine, etc., over a dish of French vanilla ice cream. Another thought is Carmen's Cordial (Page 193). Crushed fresh berries and sliced fruits in season, such as peaches are another thought. Serve with a thin, rich cookie.

ALSATIAN MOCHA CREAM

When we visited Alsace during our gastronomic tour of France, we tasted this combination and decided the Alsatians know what they're doing.

Put a couple scoops of mocha ice cream in a serving dish. Spoon over a few tablespoonfuls of prune juice. Add 4 or 5 cooked prunes (yes, the plain old stewed prunes usually eaten for breakfast) and a jigger of Eau de Vie. If you can't find Eau de Vie, try light rum.

RAINBOW PARFAIT

Layer in a parfait glass the following: a scoop of vanilla ice cream, dash of Crême de Menthe; a scoop of strawberry ice cream, a spoonful of strawberry syrup; a scoop of pineapple sherbet, a dash of Triple Sec; a swirl of whipped cream over all and a stemmed maraschino cherry or a beautiful strawberry to top it off. For kiddies, omit the booze and substitute fruit syrups.

STRAWBERRIES ROMANOFF

Choose large, perfect, fully ripe, stemmed strawberries. Soak in Curacao or Grand Marnier for 2 or 3 hours. Serve in individual dessert bowls on a "bed" of sweetened whipped cream.

STRAWBERRIES OR RASPBERRIES GRAND MARNIER

Mix 1 pint of softened French vanilla ice cream with 1 cup whipping cream, whipped. Fold in 5 tablespoons Grand Marnier. Pour over fully ripe strawberries or raspberries in individual dessert bowls. Serves 6.

COOKIES

CHOCOLATE DROP COOKIES

Here's one the grandchildren can make.

1 12-ounce package
chocolate chips
1 12-ounce package
butterscotch chips

1 #2½ can dry Chinese
noodles
1 6¾-ounce can cashew nuts

Melt chocolate and butterscotch chips over hot water. Add remaining ingredients. Drop by spoonfuls on waxpaper. Chill.

DAN'S CREAM WAFERS   2 Dozen

Former Governor Daniel Evans' **Design for Washington and Decisions for Progress** *conferences during 1965 and 1966 led to Wenatchee area citizen involvement in riverfront concern and the Riverfront Development Plan. President of Evergreen College for several years, he is chairman of the Northwest Power Planning Council.*

1 Cup soft butter
⅓ Cup whipping cream

2 Cups sifted
all-purpose flour

Mix butter, whipping cream and flour to form a soft dough. Refrigerate dough until ready to use. Remove ⅓ of dough at a time and roll out 1/8 inch thick on floured board. Cut with 1-inch round cutter. Place on ungreased cookie sheet. Prick with fork. Bake 7 to 9 minutes in 375 degree F. oven. Cool on wire racks. Sandwich 2 wafers with cream filling between.

FILLING

½ Cup softened butter
¾ Cup powdered sugar

1 Egg yolk
Rum flavoring to taste

Combine all ingredients.

BROWNIES

Like Chocolate Chip Cookies, Brownies go on forever.

1 Cup (2 cubes) butter,
  preferably unsalted
¾ Cup unsweetened cocoa
3 Large eggs
2 Cups sugar
½ Teaspoon salt

2 Teaspoons vanilla
1 Cup unbleached,
  all-purpose flour
1 Cup chopped walnuts,
  pecans or filberts

In small saucepan over low heat barely melt butter. Whisk in cocoa. Set aside to cool. Preheat oven to 350 degrees F. Butter a 9 x 13 baking pan. Or a smaller pan for a thick, cakey brownie. In medium mixer bowl beat eggs until fluffy. Gradually add sugar. Add salt and vanilla. Blend in flour alternately with cocoa mixture. Add nuts. Bake 35-40 minutes for 9 x 13 pan; or longer for smaller pan, until toothpick or cake tester comes out clean when inserted in center. Cool. Cut into squares of desired size.

CHOCOLATE CHIP COOKIES: The best recipe of all is on the Nestle chocolate chip package: The Original Toll House Cookie.

MACAROONS
Makes 2 dozen

*For years macaroons were the desserts served at the Pacific Northwest Enological Society's annual Festival dinners. Never have I tasted macaroons that equalled them, nor could I find recipes that shed any light whatsoever. During our 1980 gastronomic tour of France I tasted a macaroon here and there—just like the ones served at the Festival. Finally, here is a recipe that is **almost** like those delectable confections.*

1 Cup almond paste
¾ Cup sugar
  Pinch salt
½ Teaspoon vanilla

3 Egg whites
1 Cup flaked coconut
1 Square unsweetened
  chocolate, melted over
  hot water

Blend almond paste, sugar, salt and vanilla. I do this in my food processor; however, a mixer will do and so will manual labor, but it makes me tired to think of it. Add unbeaten egg whites, one at a time, beating well after each addition. Add coconut and mix well. Divide mixture in half. Leave one half as is. Add to the other half the melted chocolate. Let both mixtures rest for about a half-hour.

Preheat oven to 300 degrees F. Lay parchment or brown paper on baking sheets. Do not grease. Drop dough by heaping teaspoonfuls on paper, heaping them up in the center to look like Mount St. Helens. Bake 30 minutes, until just dry on the surface. Allow to cool slightly. Loosen from paper and let stand overnight, covered. They should be chewy in the center. Keep tightly covered in glass, ceramic or metal containers.

REFRIGERATOR COOKIES   Makes 6-7 dozen

I call these my basic cookies: of fine quality and perfect for any occasion calling for a cookie! Rich and delicious, they keep well. Just right with sherbet, a dish of fruit or even a glass of champagne.

3 Cups unbleached
  all-purpose flour
3½ Teaspoons baking powder
½ Teaspoon salt
1 Cup (2 cubes) butter,
  preferably unsalted

2 Cups brown sugar
2 Large eggs
1 Teaspoon vanilla
1 Cup chopped walnuts
  or pecans

Sift together flour, baking powder and salt. In a medium bowl cream butter and sugar until well blended. Add eggs and vanilla and beat until fluffy. Stir in flour mixture. Work in the chopped nuts. Form the mixture into 2 or 3 rolls 1 to 1½ inches in diameter. Wrap in wax paper and refrigerate for several hours or overnight. If you want to speed things up, place in the freezer until hardened enough to slice.

When ready to bake preheat oven to 375 degrees F. Slice dough in ¼" pieces and bake on lightly greased cookie sheets for 10 or 12 minutes. They should be a pale golden color with a caramel-colored rim. Watch carefully as they can become too brown in a flash.

"Oh weary mothers mixing dough, Don't you wish that food would grow? Your lips would smile, I know, to see A cookie bush or pancake tree!"

ISCHLER TORTCHEN

Coralie Mitterhauser was one of Columbia River Kitchen's original crew. Now living in San Francisco and teaching English riding, she is fondly remembered not only for her engaging personality, but for her Ischler Tortchen.

2½ Cups unbleached
  all-purpose flour
1 Cup (2 cubes) plus 2
  tablespoons unsalted butter
½ Cup plus 1 tablespoon sugar
¼ Cup peeled and
  ground almonds

1 Teaspoon cinnamon
Jam (raspberry is
  especially good)
Powdered sugar for
  final dusting

Preheat oven to 350 degrees F. Lightly butter a baking sheet. Crumble flour and butter. Add sugar, almonds and cinnamon. Knead mixture, then roll out to 1/8" thickness. Cut out an even number with a 3-inch cookie cutter. Make 3 small holes 3/8" in diameter in half the cookies. Bake about 12 minutes. Cool. Spread jam on cookies without holes, top with remaining cookies. Dust with powdered sugar.

RUSSIAN TEACAKES

1 Cup (2 cubes) butter,
  softened
½ Cup powdered sugar
1 Teaspoon vanilla

2¼ Cups unbleached
  all-purpose flour
¼ Teaspoon salt
¾ Cup chopped walnuts

Preheat oven to 400 degrees F. In medium bowl mix butter, powdered sugar and vanilla until creamy and smooth. Stir in flour and salt, and finally the nuts. Chill dough. Roll into balls. Roll in powdered sugar. Bake 10-12 minutes. Cool. Roll in powdered sugar again.

CAKES, FILLINGS & FROSTINGS

NELLIE CUSTIS' RECIPE
FOR A GREAT CAKE (Wrote for her Grandmamma)

This recipe came from one of the late Mrs. Rufus Woods' cookbooks. Here's something to do if you have a little spare time. "Put the whites of eggs to it, a spoonful at a time". Nellie Custis, we salute you.

Take 40 eggs and divide the whites from the yolks and beat them to a froth. Then work 4 pounds of butter to a cream and put the whites of eggs to it, a spoonful at a time, till it is well worked. Then put 4 pounds of sugar finely powdered into it, in the same manner, then put in the yolks of eggs and 5 pounds of flour and 5 pounds of fruit. Two hours will bake it. Add to it one-half an ounce of mace, one nutmeg, ½ pint of wine and some fresh brandy.

FRUITCAKE

My mother's Christmas fruitcake could be sliced paper thin. Her recipe came from Annie Black, a neighbor of Scotch ancestry.

1 ½ Cups raisins
2 Cups currants
2 Cups almonds, whole
2 Cups walnut halves
1 ½ Cups candied cherries, whole
1 Cup diced citron
½ Cup diced orange peel
¼ Cup diced lemon peel
½ Cup cubed candied pineapple

2 Cups flour
1 Cup (2 cubes) butter, preferably unsalted
1 Cup sugar
6 Large eggs
1 Teaspoon *each* cinnamon and allspice
½ Teaspoon ginger
¼ Teaspoon cloves
¼ Cup brandy

Line 2 greased 9 x 5 x 3 loaf pans with wax paper. Preheat oven to 250 degrees F.

Dredge fruits with 1 cup of the flour. Cream butter and sugar. Add eggs and brandy. Blend spices with remainder of flour and add to butter mixture. Combine with fruit. Use your hands if necessary.

Turn batter into ¾ the depth of the pans. Pack down. Decorate tops with whole fruits and nuts. Bake for 1½ hours, or until toothpick or cake tester inserted in center of the loaves comes out clean.

Bake weeks, or even months before Christmas, wrap in saran, keep in cool place, and occasionally drizzle with Madeira.

GERMAN APPLE CAKE

This super old-timer is the first to go of all the desserts at any potluck. Try it and see. Reduce sugar if desired.

2 Large eggs
1 Cup salad oil
1 Teaspoon vanilla
1½ Cups sugar
2 Cups *sifted* unbleached all-purpose flour
2 Teaspoons cinnamon
1 Teaspoon soda
¼ Teaspoon salt
4 Cups diced, tart cooking apples (Yellow Transparent, Lodi, Stayman)
1 Cup chopped walnuts

Grease and lightly dust with flour a 9 x 13 baking pan. Sift together dry ingredients. Preheat oven to 350 degrees F.

In large bowl beat eggs and oil until foamy. Add vanilla. Blend in dry ingredients well. Add apples and walnuts.

Pack into baking pan. Bake 50 to 60 minutes, or until toothpick or cake tester comes out clean when inserted in center. Cool in pan. Frost with Cream Cheese Icing. Or cut in bars and serve warm with Lemon Sauce.

CREAM CHEESE ICING

2 3-ounce packages cream cheese
3 Tablespoons melted butter
1 Teaspoon vanilla
1½ Cups powdered sugar

Soften cream cheese and mix with melted butter and vanilla. Stir in enough powdered sugar to insure good spreading consistency.

LEMON SAUCE

½ Cup sugar
1 Tablespoon cornstarch
Pinch salt
1 Cup boiling water
1½ Tablespoons lemon juice
1 Tablespoon butter

In small saucepan mix sugar, cornstarch and salt. Add boiling water gradually, stirring constantly. Place over medium heat, bring to boiling, turn down heat and simmer 5 minutes, stirring. Remove from heat. Add lemon juice and butter.

"The sweetest things are made with love".

APRICOT BABA RING

A true French baba is a yeast-bread affair, usually soaked with rum and dressed with a fruit puree. Ours is a cake baba dressed with Columbia River country apricot jam and filled with ice cream. A super dessert to crown a special dinner.

1 Cup unbleached
   all-purpose flour
1 Teaspoon baking powder
¼ Teaspoon salt
½ Cup milk
½ Cup (1 cube) butter,
   preferably unsalted
5 Egg yolks

1 Cup sugar
½ Teaspoon vanilla
1 Teaspoon grated lemon rind
2 Cups apricot jam
½ Cup light rum, warmed
   Flaked coconut
   Vanilla ice cream

Butter well a 6½-cup ring mold. Sift together flour, baking powder and salt. Preheat oven to 350 degrees F.

Heat together milk and butter until butter is melted. Remove from heat. Beat egg yolks until thick and lemon-colored. Add sugar gradually a tablespoonful at a time, beating constantly. Add vanilla and lemon rind. Add scalded milk mixture to egg yolk mixture alternately with dry ingredients. Mix until just smooth.

Pour batter into ring mold. Bake 30 or 35 minutes, or until toothpick or cake tester inserted in cake comes out clean. Cool cake 10 minutes before turning out on rack. Cool 10 minutes more before placing on rimmed cake plate.

Drizzle rum over the still warm cake. Spread on apricot jam, spooning excess around outside of ring.

When ready to serve, fill center with vanilla ice cream and sprinkle cake and ice cream with coconut.

Nadene Johnson's
MAPLE NUT CHIFFON CAKE

One of the cakes often asked for by Columbia River Kitchen customers was Nadene's recipe.

2¼ Cups unbleached
   all-purpose flour
¾ Cup sugar
1 Tablespoon baking powder
1 Teaspoon salt
¾ Cup brown sugar
½ Cup vegetable oil

5 Egg yolks
¾ Cup cold water
2 Teaspoons maple flavoring
1 Cup egg whites
½ Teaspoon cream of tartar
1 Cup finely chopped walnuts

Preheat oven to 325 degrees F. Use 10-inch angel food cake pan, making sure it is free of oil or grease.

In medium bowl sift flour, sugar, baking powder and salt. Mix in brown sugar. Make well in center and add in order: oil, egg yolks, water and flavoring. Beat until smooth. In large bowl combine egg whites and cream of tartar. Beat until stiff. Fold in carefully the flour mixture and chopped walnuts. Pour into cake pan. Bake 55 minutes. Turn up oven heat to 350 degrees and bake 10 or 15 minutes longer, until toothpick or cake tester inserted in center comes out clean. To cool, invert pan one hour. Loosen sides with a knife. Frost with Maple Icing.

MAPLE ICING
½ Cup (1 cube) butter,
   preferably unsalted
4 Cups powdered sugar

½ Cup light cream,
   or more if needed
1½ Teaspoons maple flavoring

Over medium heat in medium saucepan heat butter until melted. Blend in remaining ingredients. Place pan in ice water. Beat until of spreading consistency.

RICH CHOCOLATE CAKE

Of all the chocolate cake recipes tested, this one takes the cake. Delicious, moist, rich, light, it keeps well and is easy to make. Follow directions exactly and you cannot fail.

1 Cup unsweetened cocoa, unsifted
2 Cups boiling water
2¾ Cups *sifted,* unbleached all-purpose flour
2 Teaspoons baking soda
¼ Teaspoon salt
½ Teaspoon baking powder
1 Cup (2 cubes) butter, preferably unsalted, softened
2½ Cups sugar
4 Large eggs
2 Teaspoons vanilla

An hour before your baking is scheduled, or the night before, combine cocoa with boiling water in a small bowl. Whisk until smooth. Cool. Butter and lightly dust with cocoa three 9-inch layer-cake pans. Sift together the sifted flour, baking soda, salt and baking powder. Preheat oven to 350 degrees F.

In the large bowl of electric mixer place the butter, sugar, eggs and vanilla. Beat at high speed for 5 minutes, scraping down sides of bowl. Turn mixer to low speed and mix in the flour mixture in fourths, alternating with the cocoa mixture in thirds. Begin and end with the flour mixture. Do not overbeat.

Divide batter evenly into cake pans, bang pans on counter 2 or 3 times to remove air bubbles, and bake 35 or 40 minutes, or until a cake tester or toothpick comes out clean when inserted in center. Cool in pans 10 minutes. Loosen sides and invert on cooling rack.

RICH CHOCOLATE FILLING AND FROSTING
1 Cup (2 cubes) butter, preferably unsalted
1 Cup chocolate chips
2¼ Cups powdered sugar
2 Teaspoons vanilla
1 Large egg

In medium saucepan over hot water combine butter and chocolate chips. Stir until completely melted and smooth. Remove from heat. Add vanilla and powdered sugar. Beat until smooth. Add egg and continue beating until fluffy and stiff enough to spread.

GERMAN'S CHOCOLATE CAKE
Running neck and neck with the Rich Chocolate Cake, in my humble opinion, is German's Chocolate Cake, the recipe for which is on the wrapper of a German's chocolate bar.

The Wedding of the Year (1981) was that of Prince Charles of Great Britain and Lady "Di". Barbara Cartland, mother of Diana's step-mother received . . . "tour groups of 12 women, I believe. Those rich American widows. I shall give them tea, chocolate cake and meringues". (From a news release.)

SUPER DELUXE CHEESECAKE

This cheesecake is a variation of the one that the Columbia River Kitchen crew believed to be the most luscious and creamy ever invented. Toppings varied according to season. Sometimes it was strawberry, sometimes blueberry and sometimes lemon filling left over from the pies made for the day. The crust was always made from our bank of recycled breadcrumbs.

CRUST

1½ Cups graham cracker or vanilla cookie crumbs, *Or* recycled bread crumbs, in which case add 2 tablespoons sugar

½ Cup (1 cube) butter, preferably unsalted, melted
½ Teaspoon ginger

Mix together all ingredients and press evenly on bottom and sides of 9-inch springform pan.

FILLING

4 Large eggs
1 Cup sugar
3 8-ounce packages cream cheese
½ Cup (1 cube) butter, preferably unsalted, melted and cooled

1 Teaspoon *each* grated orange and lemon rind
½ Teaspoon vanilla

In large bowl of electric mixer beat all ingredients on medium speed for 20 minutes, until light and fluffy. Meanwhile preheat oven to 350 degrees F.

Turn mixture into prepared pan and bake 35-40 minutes. Remove from oven. Cool. Refrigerate 12 hours before serving. (If Sour Cream Topping is desired, cool only 15 minutes before spreading with topping.) When ready to serve, remove ring and finish with Strawberry Glaze.

SOUR CREAM TOPPING (optional)

2 Cups sour cream
2 Tablespoons sugar

1 Teaspoon vanilla

Mix all ingredients. Spread carefully over cheesecake, allowing a half-inch margin. Return to oven and bake 10 minutes longer.

STRAWBERRY GLAZE

4 Cups fresh strawberries,
  washed and hulled
1 Cup raspberry, strawberry
  or currant jelly

1 Tablespoon cornstarch
4 Tablespoons Cointreau or
  Grand Marnier

Dry berries completely on paper towels; otherwise, juice will ooze through the glaze. Dissolve cornstarch in liqueur. In small saucepan heat jelly. Add cornstarch mixture and continue cooking and stirring until thickened. Cool until lukewarm. Arrange berries on cake. Coat berries with glaze, allowing it to drip down sides of crust. Refrigerate until set.

PINEAPPLE UPSIDE DOWN CAKE

This old-fashioned cake is a classic, and the recipe my favorite of the several versions I have tried over the years.

10 Pineapple slices
1 Cup unbleached
  all-purpose flour
1 Teaspoon baking powder
¼ Teaspoon salt
½ Cup (1 cube) butter,
  preferably unsalted
1 Cup brown sugar

⅓ Cup walnut or pecan halves,
  or maraschino cherries
3 Large eggs
1 Cup sugar
5 Tablespoons pineapple juice
  Whipped cream for garnish

Drain pineapple slices, reserving juice. Sift together the flour, baking powder and salt. Preheat oven to 350 degrees F.

Melt butter in heavy 10-inch iron skillet. Spread with the brown sugar and remove from heat. Arrange pineapple slices over sugar. Fill centers with nut halves or maraschino cherries.

Beat eggs until light. Add sugar gradually, and then the pineapple juice alternately with dry ingredients. Blend well.

Pour batter over pineapple. Bake for 35 to 40 minutes, or until cake is golden and a toothpick inserted in the center comes out clean. Remove from oven. Allow to stand 5 minutes. Loosen cake around edges of pan. Place serving plate over the skillet and turn upside down. Lift off the skillet.

Serve cake either warm or cold, garnished with whipped cream.

SOUR CREAM BRUNCH CAKE

Bake this delectable cake ahead and freeze, if you wish. Serve it for your next kaffee klatsch.

1 Cup (2 cubes) butter, preferably unsalted
2 Cups sugar
2 Large eggs
2 Teaspoons vanilla

2 Cups *sifted,* unbleached all-purpose flour
1 Teaspoon baking powder
¼ Teaspoon salt
1 Cup sour cream
Topping

Grease well a 10-inch tube pan. Sift together flour, baking powder and salt. Preheat oven to 350 degrees F.

In large mixing bowl cream butter and sugar until well blended. Add eggs, beating until fluffy. Add vanilla and blend in. Add dry ingredients alternately with sour cream.

Combine topping ingredients until well blended. Pour ½ the batter in prepared pan. Sprinkle with ½ the topping. Add rest of the batter. Top with balance of topping mix.

Bake 1 hour and 15 minutes. Remove from oven and cool in pan for 15 minutes. Run a knife around inside of pan to loosen cake. Remove rim. Allow to cool completely. Before placing on serving plate, loosen cake around the tube and bottom. Lift off carefully.

TOPPING
¾ Cup finely chopped walnuts
¼ Cup brown sugar
1 Teaspoon cinnamon

TRIFLE

Columbia River Kitchen's Trifle only suggested the traditional British version. This astonishing creation towered at least 8 inches and was always greeted with exclamations of amazement. The basic cake can be whatever white or yellow cake you choose, be it butter, chiffon or sponge.

2 9-inch cake layers
2 Cups raspberry jam
1 Cup sherry, or ½ cup light rum or liqueur of your choice*
1 Cup raspberry juice from frozen berries, or from stewed fresh berries
1 Recipe Basic Chiffon Pie Filling (Page 182)

Fresh fruits in season, such as sliced bananas, sliced pineapple, peaches, pears and/or apricots
Berries, such as raspberries, strawberries, blueberries, blackberries and/or boysenberries
Whipped Cream Topping (Page 183)

Split each cake layer into 3, making a total of 6 thin layers. Mix sherry, rum or liqueur with raspberry juice. Prepare fruits.

Place one layer on serving plate. Spread with raspberry jam, Drizzle with raspberry juice mixture, spread with 1/5 Chiffon Pie Filling and add a layer of pineapple. Repeat with 2nd layer, jam, juice, custard and bananas and raspberries. Repeat with cake, jam, juice, custard and peaches, and so on until the 6th and top layer. Drizzle with juice mixture only. Frost top and sides with sweetened whipped cream. Garnish with jam and fruits as desired.

*See Carmen's FANTASTIC CORDIAL (Page 193).

CHOCOLATE FUDGE UPSIDE-DOWN CAKE

When this cake is baked, let it cool in the pan, turn upside-down on a serving plate—and there you are—all frosted and everything.

1 Cup unbleached, all-purpose flour
¼ Teaspoon salt
1 Teaspoon baking powder
1½ Tablespoons unsweetened cocoa
¾ Cup sugar

1 Tablespoon butter
½ Cup milk
1¼ Cups boiling water
½ Cup white sugar
½ Cup brown sugar
¼ Cup unsweetened cocoa
½ Cup chopped walnuts

Butter a 9-inch square baking pan. Sift together flour, salt, baking powder and 1½ tablespoons cocoa. Preheat oven to 350 degrees F.

Cream together the ¾ cup sugar and butter. Blend in the milk. Add dry ingredients, blending well. Pour into baking pan. Sprinkle with chopped nuts.

Mix white and brown sugars and cocoa. Sprinkle over the nuts. Pour boiling water over all and pop into the oven for 35 or 40 minutes, or until a toothpick or cake tester inserted in center comes out clean.

STRAWBERRY TORTE

Glamorous and delicious. For a Special Occasion.

1 Cup sifted cake flour	4 Egg yolks
1 Teaspoon baking powder	¼ Cup milk
¼ Teaspoon salt	1 Teaspoon vanilla
½ Cup (1 cube) butter, preferably unsalted, softened	Meringue
	Filling and Topping
½ Cup sugar	

Butter and lightly dust with flour two 9-inch cake pans. Sift together the flour, baking powder and salt. Preheat oven to 350 degrees F.

In large bowl of electric mixer place softened butter, sugar, egg yolks, milk and vanilla and beat at high speed for 5 minutes, scraping down sides of bowl occasionally. Add dry ingredients ½ at a time and blend until just smooth. Do not overbeat.

Pour into cake pans. Pile half the meringue over batter in each pan, spreading lightly and evenly. Bake 35 to 40 minutes, or until toothpick or cake tester inserted in center comes out clean and meringue is light golden in color.

Remove from oven, cool 2 or 3 minutes. Run a knife around inside of pans to loosen, and transfer to wire racks with meringue sides up. When completely cool, place on serving plate and put together with filling and topping.

MERINGUE

4 Egg whites	1 Cup sugar
¼ Teaspoon salt	1 Teaspoon vanilla
½ Teaspoon cream of tartar	

In medium bowl of electric mixer beat egg whites, salt and cream of tartar until the whites hold their peaks when beater is lifted. Add sugar a tablespoon at a time, beating after each addition until meringue is very stiff. Add vanilla.

FILLING AND TOPPING

1 Cup whipping cream	2 Cups sliced strawberries
3 Tablespoons powdered sugar	Whole strawberries for garnish

Whip cream with powdered sugar until stiff. Set aside ½. Fold sliced strawberries into other half. Spread between layers of torte, meringue sides up. Frost top with reserved whipped cream. Decorate with whole strawberries.

OLD-FASHIONED STRAWBERRY SHORTCAKE

Blueberries, blackberries, peaches, apricots, nectarines could be variations on this theme.

SHORTCAKE

2 Cups *sifted,* unbleached
   all-purpose flour
3 Teaspoons baking powder
¼ Teaspoon salt
3 Tablespoons sugar

½ Cup (1 cube) Butter,
   preferably unsalted
1 Large egg, fork beaten
1 Cup milk

Butter and lightly dust with flour a 9-inch round cake pan or 8-inch square baking pan. Preheat oven to 425 degrees F.

In medium bowl sift together the dry ingredients. Work in butter with your fingers, rubbing until consistency of giant peas. Stir in combined egg and milk until just blended.

Spread in baking pan and bake for 25 minutes, or until a toothpick or cake tester inserted' in center comes out clean. Turn out on rack to cool. Split into two layers and lift off the top. Place bottom layer, cut side up, on serving plate.

Spoon half of crushed berries on bottom layer. Replace top layer and spoon on remaining crushed berries. Spread with whipped cream and decorate with whole berries.

STRAWBERRY FILLING AND TOPPING

4 Cups strawberries,
   washed and hulled
½ Cup sugar, or to taste

1 Cup whipping cream
3 Tablespoons powdered sugar
1 Teaspoon vanilla

Reserve several of the nicer berries for garnish. Crush remainder with sugar to taste. Whip cream with powdered sugar and vanilla until stiff.

CARROT CAKE

One of the popular Columbia River Kitchen desserts was a favorite for catered box lunches. Frost or not, it's good as is.

2½ Cups unbleached
  all-purpose flour,
  or whole wheat flour
2 Teaspoons baking soda
2 Teaspoons cinnamon
½ Teaspoon salt
3 Large eggs, beaten
1½ Cups vegetable oil
1½ Cups sugar
2 Cups grated carrots, packed

1 Cup crushed pineapple,
  drained well
1 Cup chopped walnuts
1 Cup flaked coconut
2 Teaspoons vanilla
  Walnut halves and
  maraschino cherries for
  garnish (optional)

Butter and lightly dust with flour a 9 x 13 baking pan. Sift together flour, soda, cinnamon and salt. Preheat oven to 350 degrees F.

In large mixing bowl combine eggs, oil, and sugar. Blend well. Blend in flour mixture. Add carrots, pineapple, coconut, nut meats and vanilla. Pour batter into baking pan. Bake for one hour, or until cake tester or toothpick inserted in center comes out clean. Allow to cool in pan 10 minutes. Loosen edges and invert carefully on cake rack. If serving with sauce prick top of cake with fork and pour over Peggy Kells' Sauce. Or cool completely and frost with Cream Cheese Icing used for German Apple Cake recipe. Decorate with walnut halves and maraschino cherries if desired. Makes two 8½ x 4½ x 2½ loaves. Bake 1 hour at 350 degrees F. Makes three 9-inch cake layers. Bake 30 to 35 minutes at 350 degrees F.

If you wish to substitute honey for the sugar, use 1 cup. Use only 1 cup vegetable oil. Add 1 teaspoon baking powder.

PEGGY KELLS' SAUCE FOR CARROT CAKE

½ Cup buttermilk
1 Cup sugar
¼ Cup (½ cube) butter,
  preferably unsalted

1 Tablespoon white
  corn syrup
½ Teaspoon soda
1 Teaspoon vanilla

In a saucepan mix all ingredients except vanilla. Bring to boiling, reduce heat and simmer 5 minutes. Remove from heat. Add vanilla.

"For long life, eat peaches, skin and all".

FRUIT KUCHEN

Great joy prevailed on the Hobart farm when the breezes wafted the fragrance of my other's applecake to our quivering nostrils. In all of her cakes she used the heavy cream she skimmed from the milk pans in our milkhouse.

1 Recipe Shortcake   **¾ Cup sugar**
   (Page 177)   **Cinnamon, butter and other**
4 Cups sliced or halved fruit   **flavorings as suggested**

Prepare fruit and shortcake batter. Butter and lightly dust with flour a 13 x 9 x 2 baking pan. Preheat oven to 350 degrees F.

Spread batter in baking pan in a thin layer about ½ inch deep. Press fruit firmly into batter as closely together as possible, forming rows. Sprinkle with sugar, cinnamon and other flavorings as suggested. Dot with butter. Bake 35 to 45 minutes, or until fruit is tender and cake is golden brown. Serve hot or cold. Cut in squares and serve as is, with a sprinkling of powdered sugar, sweetened whipped cream, or vanilla ice cream.

APPLE KUCHEN

Select a good flavorful cooking apple such as Spitzenberg, Stayman, Golden Delicious, Jonathan, Yellow Transparent, Lodi or Gravenstein. Peel, cut into eighths. Press into dough, sprinkle with sugar, cinnamon and a grating of lemon peel. Dot with butter.

PRUNE OR NECTARINE KUCHEN

Wash fruit, cut in half and remove pits. If nectarines are large, cut in slices. Press fruit into dough in rows. Top with sugar, nutmeg and a grating of orange peel. Dot with butter.

PEACH KUCHEN

Certain varieties of peach can be peeled without blanching. If not, immerse in boiling water for a minute, peel and cut into eighths. Arrange slices in rows, pressing into dough as closely together as possible. Sprinkle with sugar, cinnamon and a grating of orange peel. Dot with butter.

PEAR KUCHEN

Peel Bartlett pears, cut in half and remove core and stem. Cut off the large rounded side and cut this piece in half. Arrange pear slices on dough, alternating large and small ends of pear, and placing the pieces between. Sprinkle with sugar, a grating of lemon peel and ½ teaspoon of anise seed. Dot with butter.

WHITE BUTTER CAKE

Wondering what to do with those extra egg whites? Make this delicate white cake, frost with 7-minute icing, and you'll never wonder again.

1 Cup (2 cubes) butter,
  preferably unsalted
1¾ Cup sugar
2 Teaspoons vanilla
1 Teaspoon almond extract
2 Cups unbleached,
  all-purpose flour

¼ Cup cornstarch
1 Tablespoon baking powder
¼ Teaspoon salt
1½ Cups milk, or more if needed
1 Cup egg whites (about 6
  large), room temperature

Grease two 9-inch layer cake pans. Cut circles of parchment or wax paper to fit bottoms, and butter. Sift together flour, cornstarch, baking powder and salt. Preheat oven to 350 degrees F.

In large mixing bowl cream butter and sugar until light and fluffy. Blend in vanilla and almond extracts. Add sifted dry ingredients alternately with milk. Blend until smooth. Beat egg whites until they hold a peak, and fold into batter carefully—up and over lightly—until just blended. Do not overmix.

Divide batter evenly into cake pans. Bang pans on counter 2 or 3 times to remove air bubbles. Bake for 35 or 40 minutes, or until a toothpick or cake tester inserted in center comes out clean. Cool in pans 5 minutes. Turn out on racks. Remove paper and cool.

SEVEN MINUTE FROSTING

Easy, fast and fail-proof, this looks like Divinity.

1½ Cups sugar
⅓ Cup water
2 Egg whites

¼ Teaspoon salt
¼ Teaspoon cream of tartar
1 Teaspoon vanilla

In top of double boiler place sugar, water, egg whites, salt and cream of tartar. Place over boiling water and beat with hand beater (preferably electric) for 7 minutes. Remove from heat. Continue beating for 5 minutes or so, until cool enough to spread. Add vanilla. Frost cake. Sprinkle with shredded coconut or chopped nuts, if desired.

PIES & PIE CRUSTS

BASIC PIE CRUST

Butter and baking powder are ingredients rarely found in piecrust recipes, but they impart an incomparable flavor and lightness.

Even though you may never have baked a pie, you will be the envy of all who taste your very first creation if you follow the simple instructions below. No matter how much you handle the dough it will never be tough. This pastry may be used for desserts, meat pies and turnovers, for quiche shells or whenever pastry is called for.

The following makes five 9-inch pie shells. May be mixed in food processor or mixer. Refrigerate or freeze what you do not use.

3 Cups unsifted, unbleached all-purpose flour
1 Teaspoon baking powder
½ Teaspoon salt
1½ Cups butter (3 cubes) preferably unsalted Do not substitute

1 Large egg
5 Tablespoons water
1 Tablespoon vinegar

Into a large bowl sift the flour, baking powder and salt. Add cold butter cut into small pieces. Using your fingers quickly work flour mixture and butter together until crumbly. (Don't let the butter melt). Make a well in the center.

Beat egg with a fork. Add water and vinegar, mix and pour into the well. Work together lightly with a fork until blended. This makes a very soft dough, so refrigerate for a half hour before rolling. Divide into equal balls. Wrap well in freezer wrap before freezing.

PREBAKED PIE SHELL

When ready to bake, preheat oven to 400 degrees F. Roll out one ball of pastry dough to fit 9-inch pie pan with outside of circle extending one inch beyond pan rim. Trim, turn under edges and crimp. Extend edge slightly over pan rim. Line shell with wax paper or parchment. Fill with beans or rice, making sure paper fits snugly against sides and bottom of pastry, with no "vacations". The purpose of this procedure is to keep the sides of pastry from collapsing into the bottom of the pan. Bake for 20 minutes. Remove from oven and lift edge of wax paper or parchment carefully to check for doneness. If bottom is still uncooked, turn down heat to 300 degrees. Remove beans or rice and paper from shell and return shell to oven to continue baking until crust is completely done.

COLUMBIA RIVER KITCHEN'S CHIFFON PIE

Next to Crab Quiche, the most asked-for recipe at Columbia River Kitchen was chiffon pie. Now the secret is out but when "butter" is indicated that's exactly what is meant. And that goes for real vanilla, and real whipped cream—not the plastic stuff sprayed from a can nor those "whips" so glamorously hawked on television.

OATMEAL CRUST
1⅓ Cups quick oats   ½ Cup brown sugar
⅓ Cup melted butter

Heat oats in shallow baking pan in 350 degree oven for 10 minutes. Combine oats, melted butter and brown sugar, mixing until crumbly. Press firmly into bottom and sides of 9-inch pie plate. Chill.

BASIC CHIFFON PIE FILLING
1¼ Cups milk, divided   1 Teaspoon cornstarch
  1 Tablespoon (1 envelope)   ½ Teaspoon salt
    gelatin   1 Cup whipping cream
  2 Large eggs, separated   1 Teaspoon vanilla
⅔ Cup sugar   1 Tablespoon sugar

Heat 1 cup of the milk in medium saucepan over medium heat. Dissolve gelatin in remaining ¼ cup. Beat egg yolks until thick and lemon-colored. Add sugar, cornstarch, salt and gelatin mixture and blend well. When milk reaches boiling point gradually add half to the egg mixture, whisking constantly. Return egg mixture to milk, stirring vigorously until thick, smooth and bubbling. Remove from heat. Chill until thickened.

When ready to assemble pie, place chilled custard mixture into medium bowl of electric mixer and beat until no lumps remain. In another bowl beat 1 cup whipping cream until stiff. Add 1 teaspoon vanilla. In a third bowl beat the two egg whites until whites hold their peaks. Add gradually 1 tablespoon of sugar until whites are stiff.

Now fold the whipped cream into the custard mixture. Then fold in the egg whites carefully. Pile into prepared shell. Chill several hours or overnight, until completely set.

WHIPPED CREAM TOPPING

1 Cup whipping cream,   ½ Teaspoon vanilla
  whipped
1 Tablespoon powdered sugar

Whip cream, add powdered sugar and vanilla. Spread on top of pie, or if you have pastry bag, pipe decorative edge and design in center. Decorate with appropriate garnish.

BANANA CREAM CHIFFON PIE

Slice 2 bananas. Arrange one in bottom of pie shell. Spoon over ½ recipe Basic Chiffon Pie Filling. Arrange other banana over filling and pile on the rest of the custard. Top with Whipped Cream Topping and garnish with chocolate curls or grated chocolate.

COCONUT CHIFFON PIE

Fold one cup flaked coconut into Basic Chiffon Pie Filling. Top with Whipped Cream Topping and garnish with ½ cup toasted coconut.

TOASTED COCONUT: Place coconut in pie pan in 350 degree F. oven. Toast a light golden brown, about 15 to 20 minutes. Watch carefully to prevent burning. Stir occasionally to allow even browning.

CHOCOLATE CHIFFON PIE

Melt 1 cup chocolate chips with 1 tablespoon unsalted butter over hot water. Cool slightly. Fold into Basic Chiffon Pie Filling. Top with Whipped Cream Topping. Garnish with grated chocolate and/or chopped walnuts.

PEANUT BUTTER CHIFFON PIE

Fold 1 cup crunchy peanut butter into Basic Chiffon Pie Filling. Top with Whipped Cream Topping. Garnish with whole peanuts.

Fayee Lafrance's

CHOCOLATE WALNUT PIE

Columbia River Kitchen's chocolate aficionados doted on Chief Baker Fayee's rich pie.

1 9-inch unbaked pie shell
(Page 181)
4 Large eggs
1 Cup unbleached
all-purpose flour
1 Cup white sugar
1 Cup brown sugar

2 Cups (1 pound) melted
butter, preferably unsalted
2 Cups chocolate chips
2 Cups chopped walnuts
Whipped cream and
chopped walnuts for garnish

Preheat oven to 350 degrees F. In large bowl of mixer beat eggs until foamy. Beat in flour, white and brown sugars. Blend in melted butter. Stir in chocolate chips and nuts. Pour in prepared shell. Bake one hour, until set in center. Cool. Decorate with whipped cream. If you have pastry bag, pipe decorative design and sprinkle with chopped walnuts.

WILD BLACKBERRIES—ONLY A MEMORY?

One of the earliest memories of my childhood on the Hobart farm was the annual blackberry picking expedition led by my mother and father, with my sister, brother and I crying and complaining in their wake—across the swamp on our land to the hill beyond. The day-long ordeal, often in the hot sun, was mercifully broken at noon with a banquet of fried chicken, potato and vegetable salads, homemade bread and home-churned butter sandwiches and lemonade. We did not return home until our 4 milk buckets were full of berries and it was time for the evening milking.

Our gloom was transformed to joy as we helped my mother "pick over" the berries preparatory to canning them. Visions of blackberry shortcake with whipped cream, blackberry pie, hotcakes with black-berries and whipped cream, and just plain dishes of berries with sugar and thick cream triggered such serious cases of mouth watering that only frequent ministrations of blackberries could affect a cure.

Blackberries and blackcaps can be found in Columbia River Country, but one must be alert and crafty if one is to get a gallon or so for the freezer. Patches are closely guarded secrets. Keeping an eye on the progress of logged and burned-over areas near Lake Wenatchee and Lake Chelan, and making spot checks around July 4 can be helpful. The Wenatchee World runs reports on the status of blackberry and huckleberry patches. With our Lake Wenatchee cabin as a base, we planned on starting for the patch after sunrise on Wednesdays, before the weekend rush.

WILD BLACKBERRY PIE

The following pastry is good with all berry and fruit pies.

GALETTE DOUGH

1½ Cups unbleached all-purpose flour	1 Egg yolk
½ Teaspoon salt	1½ Tablespoons water
1 Tablespoon sugar	1½ Tablespoons lemon juice
½ Cup (1 cube) butter, preferably unsalted	

Work butter into sifted dry ingredients. Mix with a fork the egg yolk, water and lemon juice. Work rapidly into the first mixture until it holds together. Roll out and line a 9-inch pie pan. Cut remainder of dough in ½-inch strips and make lattice-work covering for the following filling:

FILLING

4 Cups blackberries, boysenberries, raspberries, strawberries, huckleberries or blueberries	¾-1 Cup sugar, depending on sweetness of berries
	¼ Cup flour
	1 Teaspoon lemon juice

Preheat oven to 450 degrees F. Sprinkle lemon juice over berries. Mix flour and sugar and blend carefully into berries. Fill pie crust, top with lattice (full crust may also be used). Place pan on bottom rack of oven and bake for 10 minutes. Turn down heat to 350 degrees and bake about 40 minutes longer, or until berries are bubbling through the top. Serve with whipped cream.

GLAZE: If full top crust is used, brush with a fork-beaten egg before placing in oven.

Lorna Larsen's

FRESH RASPBERRY PIE

Lorna's husband, Paul, superintendent of the Tree Fruit Research Center, distinguished himself as the first chairman of Community Development Council, citizen arm for implemetation of the River-front Development Plan. Her pie caused a sensation in our family.

1 Prebaked 8-inch pie shell (Page 182)	Dash salt
1½ Cups water	4 Tablespoons water
3½ Cups fresh raspberries	1 Tablespoon lemon juice (optional)
¾ Cup sugar	1 Cup whipping cream
3 Tablespoons cornstarch	

Boil together for one minute the water and ½ cup of the raspberries. Strain. Discard seeds. Mix to a paste the sugar, cornstarch, salt, 4 tablespoons water and lemon juice. Pour the raspberry juice into a saucepan, bring to boiling and add the cornstarch mixture. Cook until thick. Cool to lukewarm and "runny". Add the 3 cups of fresh raspberries. Turn into baked pie shell. Chill. When ready to serve top with whipped cream, sweetened with powdered sugar, if desired.

Mary Harmon's

FRESH STRAWBERRY PIE

Assistant Baker Mary's contribution to Columbia River Kitchen's tempting array of pies was this beautiful and popular creation.

1 Prebaked 9-inch pie shell (Page 182)	1 3-ounce package strawberry gelatin
2 Cups water	4 Cups sliced fresh strawberries
1½ Cups sugar	
6 Drops red food coloring	Whipped cream and whole berries for garnish
3 Tablespoons cornstarch	

In small pan mix 1 cup of the water, sugar and food coloring. In a small bowl mix remaining water with the cornstarch. Bring water and sugar mixture to boiling. Add cornstarch mixture, stirring constantly, and cook until thickened. Remove from heat. Add strawberry gelatin and dissolve completely. Place sliced berries in pie shell. Pour syrup over. Refrigerate. When set, garnish with whipped cream and whole berries.

DANISH APPLE PIE

This recipe is adapted from a dessert enjoyed in Hotel Scandinavia's restaurant in Copenhagen. Made by 18 year-old chef Sylvia Hansen of Finland, it was served in individual baking dishes. Columbia River Kitchen served it as a pie. Here is another use for those recycled bread crumbs. Easy to make, inexpensive and glamorous.

4 Cups applesauce, made of summer apples such as Yellow Transparent, Lodi, or Spitzenberg; or other flavorful apples such as Gravenstein, Stayman, Jonathan or Golden Delicious. Sugar to taste
2 Teaspoons vanilla

2 Cups dried breadcrumbs
½ Cup (1 cube) melted butter, preferably unsalted
Cinnamon
Whipped cream, sweetened to taste with powdered sugar
Jelly or jam for garnish: raspberry, strawberry, apricot, currant

Butter a 9-inch deep-dish glass pie plate. Preheat oven to 350 degrees F. Pat ⅓ of the crumbs on the bottom of pie plate. Layer with ⅓ of the applesauce. Sprinkle with cinnamon. Repeat, finishing with bread-crumbs on top. Pour melted butter over the crumbs, saturating them, at the same time poking with a skewer to allow butter to run down through the pie.

Bake 40 minutes. Cool. Run knife around inside of the pie plate to loosen. Top with sweetened whipped cream. Decorate lavishly with whatever kind of jelly or jam you happen to have around the house.

FRENCH OR STREUSEL FRUIT PIES

The streusel fresh fruit pies were a great favorite at Columbia River Kitchen's booth at the early Apple Valley Street Fairs, during the days before a restaurant was established across from the Clinic on 9th Street.

Tree-ripened North Central Washington soft fruits burst with juice— to prevent a soggy bottom crust use a good quality aluminum pie pan. Disposable aluminum pans should be punched full of holes to allow immediate influx of heat. Glass pie plates are not advised unless crust is prebaked, and this is possible. Serve with whipped cream or vanilla ice cream if desired.

STREUSEL TOPPING

To save time make up a batch big enough for 5 pies. Refrigerate or freeze in covered glass, ceramic or stainless steel containers. Use 1½ cups for each 9-inch pie.

4 Cups unsifted, unbleached all-purpose flour
4 Cups brown sugar, packed
1 Cup (2 cubes) softened butter, preferably unsalted

½ Teaspoon salt
2 Teaspoons cinnamon

In a bowl combine all ingredients. Rub mixture quickly through your fingers until thoroughly blended and crumbly.

FRENCH APRICOT, NECTARINE OR PEACH PIE

1 9-inch unbaked pie shell (Page 181)
4 Cups pitted, halved apricots, halved or sliced nectarines, or sliced peaches

¾ Teaspoon grated orange peel
1½ Cups Streusel Topping

Preheat oven to 400 degrees F. Sprinkle ¼ cup Streusel Topping in bottom of pie shell. Arrange fruit over Topping: halved apricots and nectarines, if small, with cut sides up. Mix orange peel with remainder of Topping. Sprinkle Topping evenly over fruit, patting lightly to pack down.

Place pan on bottom rack of oven. Bake for 20 minutes. Reduce heat to 375 degrees F. Continue baking for 20 or 25 minutes, or until fruit is tender and bubbling. Cool.

SOUR CHERRY OR RHUBARB PIES

Add ¾ to 1 cup of sugar to fruit before placing in pie shell. Add ½ teaspoon almond flavoring to Sour Cherry filling.

FRENCH PEAR PIE

1 9-inch unbaked pie shell (Page 181)	3 Tablespoons thawed frozen orange juice concentrate
4 Large fresh Bartlett pears	1½ Cups Streusel Topping

Preheat oven to 400 degrees F. Sprinkle ¼ cup Topping in bottom of pie shell. Peel, core and slice pears thinly. Toss lightly with undiluted orange juice concentrate. Arrange in pie shell. Sprinkle Topping evenly over fruit, patting lightly to pack down. Follow baking instructions for French Apricot, nectarine or Peach Pie.

FRENCH APPLE PIE

Columbia River Kitchen's French Apple Pies were made with Golden Delicious apples, precooked in huge quantities. Prepare filling in advance, if desired, refrigerate and bring to room temperature before pouring into pie shell. A top crust could be substituted for Streusel Topping. This recipe was featured in the national Family Weekly newspaper supplement.

1 9-inch unbaked pie shell (Page 181)	⅓ Cup sugar
7 Cups sliced Golden Delicious apples (sliced ½-inch thick)	¼ Teaspoon salt
	1 Teaspoon vanilla
	½ Teaspoon grated lemon rind
1¼ Cups water	1½ Cups Streusel Topping (Page 188)
4 Teaspoons quick-cooking tapioca	

In medium saucepan combine apples, water, tapioca, sugar and salt. Bring to boiling, reduce heat and simmer until apples are almost tender and tapioca is transparent. Remove from heat. Cool 20 minutes. Add vanilla. Preheat oven to 400 degrees F. Mix grated lemon rind with topping. Pour cooked apple mixture in pie shell. Arrange Topping evenly over filling.

Place pan on bottom rack of oven. Bake 20 minutes. Reduce heat to 375 degrees F. and continue baking 20 minutes, or until mixture bubbles in the center of the pie. Cool.

NEW ENGLAND APPLESAUCE PIE

Substitute 1 cup seedless raisins for 2 cups sliced uncooked apples in above recipe.

LEMON MERINGUE PIE

Columbia River Kitchen's Lemon Meringue Pie was always guaranteed to stop the show when the restaurant's original Chief Baker, Florence Orndoff, brought it up from the basement bakeshop. But like most good things, it isn't cheap. The following quantities are given for one 9-inch pie, but the recipe was always doubled, so that 8 egg whites crowned this stunning creation.

1 Pre-baked 9-inch pie shell (Page 182)
1½ Cups water
1½ Cups sugar
½ Teaspoon salt
¼ Cup cornstarch
⅓ Cup cold water

4 Large eggs, separated
½ Cup freshly squeezed lemon juice (*not* bottled, reconstituted juice)
1 Teaspoon grated lemon rind
4 Tablespoons butter (optional)

In large saucepan bring 1½ cups water, sugar and salt to boiling. Meanwhile, in medium bowl of electric mixer (or by hand) blend thoroughly the cornstarch, ⅓ cup cold water, egg yolks, lemon juice and lemon rind. Pour gradually into boiling sugar-water mixture, stirring vigorously until mixture is bubbly and clear. Remove from heat. Add butter. Cool to lukewarm. Pour into pie shell. Preheat oven to 350 degrees F.

Mound meringue quickly on pie, making sure that edges all around the pie are sealed. Now do your thing and make the meringue look like Mount St. Helens before the eruption. Bake 12 to 15 minutes, or until meringue is a rich golden color. Cool thoroughly before serving.

MERINGUE
4 Egg whites
¼ Teaspoon Cream of Tartar

½ Cup sugar

In medium bowl of electric mixer beat egg whites and cream of tartar until whites hold their peaks when beater is lifted. Add sugar a tablespoonful at a time, beating thoroughly after each addition until meringue is very stiff.

PUMPKIN CHIFFON PIE

Another one of Columbia River Kitchen's great pie successes. If you like to be showered with compliments, bake this pie.

1 Pre-baked 9-inch pie shell
  (Page 182)
1 Tablespoon (1 envelope)
  gelatin
¼ Cup cold water
3 Large eggs, separated
1 Cup sugar
1⅓ Cups cooked pumpkin

⅓ Cup milk
½ Teaspoon salt
1 Teaspoon, mace
1 Teaspoon vanilla
1½ Cups whipping cream
¾ Cup flaked coconut,
  toasted (Page 183)

Soften gelatin in cold water. In top of double boiler beat egg yolks until thick and lemon-colored. Add ½ cup of the sugar, pumpkin, milk, salt and mace, place over boiling water and cook until thick, stirring constantly. Remove from heat. Add softened gelatin and stir until dissolved. Cool. Add vanilla.

Beat egg whites at high speed until peaks form when beater is raised. Add remaining ½ cup sugar a tablespoonful at a time, beating after each addition until stiff. Fold into cooled pumplin mixture. Beat ½ cup of the cream until stiff. Fold into pumpkin mixture.

Spoon into baked pie shell. Chill several hours or overnight. When ready to serve beat remaining 1 cup cream until stiff. Spread on top of filling. Sprinkle with toasted coconut.

PUMPKIN PIE: In my humble opinion, the best recipe for the conventional pumpkin pie is on the Libby pumpkin can.

CORDIALS, WINES & CONFECTIONS

KAHLUA

Make at least 2 weeks before you need it. Of course you can buy Kahlua at the liquor store, but it's a lot less expensive this way.

4 Cups water
4 Cups sugar
2 Ounces instant coffee
  (Antiqua is good)

2 Vanilla beans, split
  lengthwise
1 Fifth Vodka or brandy

Mix sugar and water. Boil 5 minutes. Add instant coffee. Mix well. Pour in gallon jug. Add vanilla beans (supermarket or health food store) and Vodka or brandy. Let stand 2 weeks. Serve as liqueur, flavoring or topping for vanilla ice cream.

LOVE POTION   Serves 2

If all else fails, this might work.

2 Scoops vanilla ice cream
½ Ounce *each* Drambuie and
  Grand Marnier

Dash of Grenadine

Place all ingredients in blender and whip until liquified.

A DRINK A DAY KEEPS THE DOCTOR AWAY

*Drinking for "medicinal purposes" is back in style. A recent study to learn about the eating and drinking habits of middle-aged men revealed that the consumption of alcoholic beverages may supply some necessary nutrients—niacin, riboflavin and phosphorus—missing in non-drinkers' diets. Also revealed—a moderate intake of alcohol guards against coronary heart disease, perhaps because of the moderate drinker's greater number of high-density lipoproteins, the **good** cholesterol that guards against clogging arteries. Booze reduces tension, lowers the pulse rate and induces sleep, especially among the elderly, according to the study.*

DANDELION WINE

"A waltz and a glass of wine invite an encore" . . . *Johann Strauss.*

Each year my mother made a batch of dandelion wine which she stored in the basement of our home on the Hobart farm. Now and then she brought up a bottle for either "medicinal purposes" or to serve on special occasions in tiny liqueur glasses.

We kids were assigned the ordeal of picking the blossoms, and earned our reward: the joy of drinking in the aroma of oranges and lemons as my mother sliced them for the wine. Oranges were a luxury in those days.

Dandelion blooms should be picked on a dry, sunny morning preferably on or about April 23. Taking a hint from the Swiss whose cows are not permitted to graze on dandelion meadows defiled by fertilizers (it would make their Emmental Cheese taste bitter and age improperly), I pick only the blossoms flourishing on virgin soil.

4 Quarts dandelion blossoms, all traces of stem removed	6 Cups sugar
4 Quarts boiling water	3 Sliced oranges
1 Tablespoon wine yeast or baker's yeast	3 Sliced lemons

Pick full and newly-opened blooms. Pour boiling water over flowers and allow to stand 24 hours. Strain into a crock or glass container. Add all remaining ingredients, cover with towel and let stand 9 days, stirring once each day.

Siphon into a gallon jug, cap loosely and keep filled brim full with water until fermentation has ceased and wine is clear—about 3 weeks. Bottle, cork and store in a cool place until Christmas.

CARMEN'S CORDIAL

Make 10 days before needed. Place in a quart jar 2 cups crushed ripe berries: raspberries, strawberries, blackberries or boysenberries. Add ½ cup sugar. Fill with vodka. Cover tightly. Turn over each day for 10 days. Strain and bottle. Serve as a liqueur or as a sauce over French vanilla ice cream.

MAPLE SUGAR

Archie Marlin, who with his wife operates The Alps in Tumwater Canyon, contributed this recipe from his "Rigby's Reliable Candy Maker". Archie makes wonderful candies including super peanut brittle.

This is a good substitute for maple sugar and is about as good and about as pure as we usually get.

Break up in small pieces all the corn cobs you can get into a large kettle, now put all the water you can get in with them and boil good for two hours. Let stand over night, then skim off the water and add 16 pounds of the darkest brown New Orleans sugar to each gallon of water and cook to 250. Set it off and with a paddle stir it until it starts to grain, then put it in pie pans, cups, bread pans, saucers, or in fact anything to make it look as if it was made in the country by an honest farmer. When all is grained it can be turned out of the pans or dishes and is ready for the store, with the usual sign "Pure Maple Sugar".

MOTHER NATURE

MOTHER NATURE

APPLES, APPLE CIDER AND VINEGAR

"An apple a night makes dentists' bills light. An apple a day keeps the doctor away".

"In apples nature has imprisoned a lime, which nourishes and builds up our bones: iron, magnesium and sulphur which purify the blood, clear the skin and assist the bowels; phosphorous which is a great nerve tonic; and other medicinal properties highly conducive to good health. Apples are nature's tonic. They stimulate the appetite, aid digestion and tone up and strengthen the entire system".

—From a 1930 cookbook compiled by ladies of the First Methodist Church Wesleyan Guild

Besides the minerals pinpointed by the Methodist ladies, apples are rich in potassium necessary for growth; chlorine, sodium, fluorine silicon and many trace minerals. Apple cider and apple cider vinegar contain most of the same minerals.

According to the Washington State Apple Commission, the climate and soil in Washington's appleland is perfect for growing apples. The soil is deep fertile volcanic ash, deposited millions of years ago. This productive earth is rich in minerals on which apples thrive, making Washington apple trees some of the most productive in the world.

Controlled atmosphere storage (CA) makes it possible to enjoy freshly picked apples all year round. In CA storage the oxygen in the air around the apples is decreased and a higher concentration of carbon dioxide substituted, thereby lowering the apples' breathing rate.

RED DELICIOUS: For salads and eating as is.

GOLDEN DELICIOUS: Best all-purpose. For salads, cooking, baking and eating as is.

ROME: The perfect baking apple.

McINTOSH: For applesauce and crunching.

STAYMAN: All-purpose cooking and eating.

GRANNY SMITH: All-purpose cooking and baking. Tart.

LODI AND YELLOW TRANSPARENT: Summer apples. Wonderful for applesauce and green apple pies.

NEWTOWN: All-purpose cooking and baking.

JONATHAN: All-purpose cooking and eating.

To top off all its virtues, the average-sized apple weighing approximately 150 grams, contains only 80 calories.

ASPARAGUS

Did you know that asparagus is a sedative? (It's also a diuretic). This superb vegetable is prevalent in orchards and along roadways around Apple Blossom Time. So! Let's throw away the tranquilizers, get on our old clothes and gather some for dinner. Plenty of smart people will have beat us to it, you can be sure of that.

To prepare, simply cut off the toughest part of the stem, place in a saucepan, add a little salt and a half cup or so of water, bring to boiling, reduce heat and steam until tender, around 8 to 10 minutes. Remove carefully with slotted spoon or pancake turner, place in serving dish, add butter liberally and serve.

To serve as a salad, chill and serve with your favorite dressing.

If you're using "store-bought" asparagus, cut off the white butt end, about an inch or so, and peel skin up to where the green begins, thereby salvaging a good proportion of the stalk through this tenderization process.

ASPARAGUS EGGS BENEDICT (Page 87).

VINEGAR

Besides being a powerhouse of potassium and an important part of our diet through salads and other dishes, vinegar is a valuable ally in household chores.

Vinegar cleans the steam iron and coffee pot, washes windows, loosens the limestone deposit in the toilet bowl, cleans soap scum off shower tiles and doors, removes onion, fish odors and fruit stains from your hands, holds together the egg white when you poach eggs. How versatile can you get!

Vinegar is very easy to make. Just buy a jug or two of natural apple cider (unpasteurized) and allow it to be exposed to the air by unscrewing the cap just enough so the jug will not be airtight. When the cider has turned to vinegar, strain and rebottle.

PIONEER VINEGAR (from Marge Klingenberg)

In covered wagon days every family carried 2 or 3 five-gallon kegs of molasses. As soon as they located anywhere, a keg was emptied and vinegar started by filling the keg with water, leaving in about a pint of molasses and a yeast cake soaked soft. A piece of coarse brown paper 8 inches square, smeared with molasses was added. The keg was covered with cloth and set in the sun, where it soon soured and made good vinegar. All emptied fruit and jelly glasses, and cups with sugar in bottoms were rinsed and added. As there was no fruit, it was welcome.

THE LOVELY DANDELION

My mother served dandelion greens in the Spring as a "blood tonic". (Another of her tonics was sulphur and molasses, a real horror). We 3 kids had the job of digging up the greens, and as usual, complained bitterly of such abuse.

The dandelion's botanical name, Taraxacum officinale, means "official remedy for disorders". American Indians used the juice of the root for kidney ailments. Healers have used it to cure insomnia and nervousness (now called "tension").

It's said that the Romany Gypsies who live in the New Forest of England use the dandelion for its medicinal properties—for the treatment of diabetes, anemia and all kinds of kidney problems.

Angelo Pellegrini, Professor of English at the University of Washington and a noted gourmet, sings the praises of the dandelion as an accompaniment to a good roast, steak or chops, to be relished with a good bottle of Napa Valley Cabernet Sauvignon.

We attended the International Gastronomic Festival in Dijon during our October tour of the wine valleys of France, and tasted the fabulous Swiss Emmental cheese, cut from huge wheels. The cows responsible for this cheese graze on dandelion meadows undefiled by fertilizers and pesticides.

DANDELION SALAD

Serve this vitamin-rich green, unsurpassed source of Vitamin A and iron, as a salad with French dressing. Or mix the leaves with other salad greens. Snip them in every day along with fresh herbs from your garden: chives, oregano, parsley, marjoram, etc.

WILTED DANDELION GREENS

My mother served the first, fresh spears of green in Spring. Wilt greens by pouring boiling water over them. Drain off water immediatedly to remove bitterness. Add just barely enough water to keep from drying out and burning and steam, covered, until tender—about 3 or 4 minutes. Serve with cream and a sprinkling of chopped hard-cooked egg. Have a cruet of vinegar handy.

So—next time you have the urge to stamp out the pest in your lawn, remember the Romany Gypsies, the American Indians, and the Swiss who make that wonderful cheese!

HOMEMADE COTTAGE CHEESE, BUTTER, SOUR CREAM AND OTHER GOOD THINGS

There are times, such as when I open a carton of modern sour cream, when I realize how fortunate we were to have those beautiful Guernsey cows on the Hobart farm. (We kids certainly didn't think so when we had to do the chores necessary for their maintenance—feeding, herding and helping with the raking, piling and hauling of hay for winter fodder—to say nothing of the milking).

Each day a quantity of milk was set aside in our milkhouse for family use, and the rest run through the separator. Skim milk went to the pigs, some cream was saved for butter, and the rest went into the cans for the creamery.

One of the jobs we passed around was churning the butter, then washing and salting in a huge wooden bowl using a wooden paddle. The buttermilk is unforgettable: thick with globs of butter floating in it.

From time to time a big pan of milk, covered with a cloth, sat in a warm place near our kitchen stove, waiting to sour. When it had clabbered my mother would put it in a cheesecloth bag to drain and later mix it with cream, salt and chopped chives. And there was our cottage cheese.

We often had buttermilk or clabbered milk (our "yogurt") for lunch with hot, boiled potatoes.

Indoctrinated in my mother's conviction that pasteurized milk is "dead food" I searched and found raw milk in Wenatchee all during our children's growing-up years. Today it is available in supermarkets, thanks to today's growing nutrition awareness.

DILL

Dill was used by ancient Greeks and Romans for garlands to crown their conquering heroes.

During Colonial times people took "meeting seeds" to church, chewing them in an effort to stay awake. Caraway, fennel and dill were popular.

This versatile herb is marvelous with cucumbers, tomatoes, potato salad, buttered new potatoes, green salads, fish, egg dishes, pickles, stews and cottage cheese. Excellent with leaf lettuce.

Toss a few seeds among your zinnias and back of the tomato plants. They're self-maintaining. Dry the stalks and seeds for your winter seasoning needs.

PARSLEY

A healthful and flavorful asset to salads, soups, meat and vegetable dishes. So scatter a few seeds among your petunias, and then let a plant or two go to seed. Dry what you don't need immediately during the hot summer months, store in jars and you'll have a plentiful supply all year.

Parsley is loaded with Vitamin A, and according to an old herbal, wonderful for falling sickness and bad breath! Dieters note: it's a diuretic.

ROSEMARY

Let's make some Rosemary Tea and activate our sluggish brains! It's supposed to help a weak memory and quicken the senses. Rosemary comforts the stomach, rests the heart, benefits the gums and teeth, helps digestion and drives away flatulence.

I tried some tea for my memory, but one dose didn't seem to help. Think I'll try it again, though.

Remember the benefits of Rosemary as you season your salmon, venison, beef, lamb, pork, veal, chicken, duck, pheasant and quail. Use it in chicken soup, in peas, potatoes and mushrooms.

HONEY

One of the important Fall happenings of my childhood was the robbing of the beehives. In retrospect, my father resembled a modern-day spaceman in his costume of protective clothing and equipment, which included a beehat and veil, gloves and smoker.

As my mother cut the honeyladen wax from the frames to drain for storage in fruit jars, we kids waited for sticky mouthfuls of honey and beeswax, which soon dwindled to just beeswax. I think we chewed it for days.

Fruitgrower-beekeepers are legion in North Central Washington. Bees are important to the fruit industry.

An expert beekeeper is Glenn Crawford, Wenatchee florist. Glenn came from the midwest where his family gathered honey from honeytrees. An experimenter with various grasses in his cherry and apple orchards in his search for varieties of honey flavors, he is a skillful trapper of swarming bees.

Dr. Gordon Congdon advises that honey is high in Potassium, thought England consider the combination of honey and garlic the elixir of claimed to be a mild laxative; soothing to a cough and contributing to the relief from the pain of arthritis.

HONEY AND ALLERGIES: Glenn maintains that if you eat the honey of bees gathering nectar within 2 miles of your residence, you'll suffer no allergies from weeds in that radius.

NATURE'S SEDATIVE: Stir a tablespoonful of honey into a cup of hot milk, and drink before you turn in.

HANGOVER PREVENTATIVE AND REMEDY: Eat 1 tablespoonful honey prior to indulgence. Or equal parts of honey and grapefruit juice after the last drink.

ELIXIR OF YOUTH: The Romany Gypsies of the New Forest of England consider the combination of honey and garlic the elixir or youth, I've heard.

SHE KNOWS WHAT SHE'S TALKING ABOUT

Barbara Cartland, British novelist at 79 appears 20 years younger. Her special interest besides romance, the gypsies and old-age pensioners is nutrition. "You'll never get an exciting, virile husband out of a paper bag," says she.

THE SPRING

In the days before our well and the pump on our back porch, all the water we used came from a spring adjoining a creek across the railroad tracks. We kids had the job of carrying water in milk buckets —quite a job on wash day. How we cried!

Installed over the spring was a box built by my father. In it, before we built our milkhouse, we kept our milk, butter and cream icy cold. An added bonanza were the crayfish that congregated in the corners and walls of the box. Much to their sorrow, they wound up as another delicacy for the supper table: boiled, removed from their shells and doused in melted butter.

MUSHROOM HUNTERS

The first Fall rains of my childhood heralded the arrival of the mushroom hunt, and my Austrian mother and we 3 trailers would be gleefully off to the woods in back of our barn to search among the fir needles for the furry, black buttons and the dark brown caps which she called "health", but which were really Boletus. We also gathered the purple Russula because it was there, but we really didn't like it very well. It was a bit too peppery.

In the Spring we gathered Morels, though not as enthusiastically, and through the Summer the beautiful creamy and delicious Agaricus Augustus—which we called the meadow mushroom. But the real prize was the Boletus. In Europe it is considered among gourmets to be very close to the truffle in flavor.

My sister and brother follow the pattern of our childhood, and in the wake of the Fall rains range the fir forests out of Renton and North Bend—to bring home buckets of Boletus, and to can them, using my mother's method, and to store them for the wonderful wintertime dishes to come.

CANNED BOLETUS MUSHROOMS

Remove forest debris. Trim stems and discolored parts. Cut sponge from older mushrooms. Leave the button-size whole. Dice and boil 3 minutes in salted water—about a teaspoonful to a quart. Drain. Rinse with cold water until mushrooms are cool. Pack loosely in ½-pint jars. Add ¼ teaspoon salt, cover and seal. Process 3 hours in hot water bath. Process at 10 pounds for 15 minutes if using pressure cooker.

MORELS

Tiny Ardenvoir on the Entiat River, a tributary of the Columbia, escaped one of the disastrous fires which swept forests of the Cascades in 1970—destroying natural beauty for a generation to come.

Morel mushrooms have a place in the regeneration of fire-ravaged earth, for they rise the like the mythical Phoenix from the ash. They also like pastures, fields and roadsides.

True to the prediction of Ellis and Mabel Miller, they abounded on the creeks flowing into the Entiat, attracting mushroom hunters statewide. The Millers also found Morels on the Cooper Mountain and Gold Ridge burns near Lake Chelan.

Cut off bulbous end, if dirty. Rinse out the pockets under running water, if necessary. Drain. To cook, dip in beaten egg, then in cracker crumbs and fry quickly in butter until golden brown.

Amy Miller's

CHANTERELLES

Amy, whose husband is Dr. C. K., is considered North Central Washington's expert on mushrooms. She finds Chanterelles near Lake Wenatchee beginning in September on into the Fall.

She simply sautes Chanterelles in butter and says they hardly ever reach the table.

RUSSIAN STYLE MUSHROOM SOUP (Page 32).
Carmen's SCRAMBLED EGGS AND MUSHROOMS (Page 87).
STUFFED MUSHROOMS (Page 123).
PICKLED MUSHROOMS (Page 8).

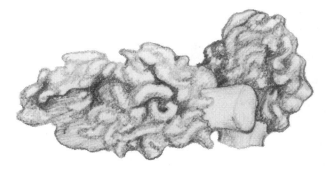

Al Brandt's

SAUERKRAUT

Sauerkraut is an ancient food that had its beginnings in the Third Century BC in China during the building of the Great Wall. Sauerkraut supplemented rice in the workers' daily rations. Roving Tartars carried it to the western part of Europe now known as Germany, where it was named.

Sauerkraut's Vitamin C kept early 18th century seamen free of scurvy. It is rich in Vitamins B1 and B12, Calcium and Phosphorus, and to top it all off—it's low in calories.

Every fall a looked-forward-to event on the Hobart farm was the annual pilgrimage to Kent for a load of late October cabbage (the same Kent of rich black farmland now part of the Kent-Auburn concrete jungle). The enthusiasm engendered by the trip waned as elbow-grease time approached: shredding the cabbage for the crock.

My brother carries on the ritual, and we are the lucky beneficiaries at Christmas.

**40 Pounds sound
      cabbage heads**   **1 Pound coarse salt**

Remove outer disreputable leaves. Quarter, remove cores and shred, using cabbage shredder. Mix 5-pound batches with 2 ounces salt each. Pack down *firmly* in a crock. Weigh down with upside-down plate topped with a large rock or a gallon jug filled with water, allowing juice to come up over the plate. Cover with a clean cloth and store in a cool spot.

Sauerkraut should be cured in about 30 days (and the distinctive odor of the curing process won't let you forget it) when the kraut will be translucent and level of the brine, which should be milky, will have dropped. If scum forms, skim it off.

When cured, pack kraut in quart jars. Add brine of 2 tablespoons salt to one quart water, filling jars to ½ inch of top. Seal jars and boil 10 minutes in hot water bath. Cool and store.

PIONEER MEDICINE

Following the revelation of Acupuncture in Chinese medical use, a prominent American physician predicted that herbal remedies would be the next medicinal import from China. Time does alter things. A few years back herbal remedies were looked upon in the same suspicious light as natural foods.

During our growing years my mother nursed us during convalescenses with drinks of hot milk and honey. Colds were treated with scalding foot baths accompanied by hot lemonade, and reinforcements from the teakettle came unrelentingly until the desired "sweat" was achieved. The worst thing of all was the dreaded dose of senna leaves tea.

Bill Robler of Carlton up the Methow River, told of remedies used by the Colville Indians:

TO STOP BLEEDING AND HEAL OPEN SORES: Powder from puffballs.

DYSENTARY: Tea from the roots of wild roses.

CATHARTIC: Tea from the roots of the Oregon Grape.

To avoid starvation when lost at high elevations, eat baked moss.

LOTS OF CHICKENS AND LOTS OF POTATOES

During 1973 hides from freshly killed pigs were flown to a Wenatchee hospital from the Burn Treatment Skin Bank in Phoenix to treat a badly burned child. The nation's largest burn center is located in Seattle—the University of Washington Regional Burn Center at Harborview Medical Center. Recently, a revolutionary discovery in burn medicine was revealed—a synthetic skin to treat severe burns. A far cry from pioneer days.

Ann (Greer) Baker, one of 9 children who grew up on a ranch on the Entiat River recalls: "When accidents happened, we may not have had medicine or drugs on hand—and we may have been too far from a doctor or hospital to get help, but we had lots of chickens and lots of potatoes".

FOR CUTS: Ann was where she shouldn't have been when a pony's kick resulted in a badly gashed lip. Her mother broke an egg, peeled the membrane from the inside, and plastered it over the gash. As the egg white dried, it drew the cut edges together tightly. Result: No scar.

FOR BURNS: Standing on an apple box to snitch something from the warming oven, Ann fell on the wood stove, burning her entire right side. Her father grated potatoes and plastered the burned areas. As the potatoes turned black he removed them, repeating the process until the potatoes no longer turned black. Result: No scars.

THERE'VE BEEN SOME CHANGES MADE
WENATCHEE WORLD PRESS RUN, June 20, 1981—A common scene now that the importance of regular exercise along with proper nutrition is recognized in the maintenance of good health. Just a few years ago a jogger was suspected of being a little off his or her rocker.

MAIL ORDER FORM

Please send me _____ copies of THE COLUMBIA RIVER COOKBOOK. I enclose $10.95 plus $1.50 shipping/handling for each copy. Washington residents add applicable sales tax. Ship book(s) to:

_____
Name

_____
Address

_____   _____   _____
City   State   Zip

Mail Form To: Columbia River Press, Box 1647, Wenatchee, WA 98801

MAIL ORDER FORM

Please send me _____ copies of THE COLUMBIA RIVER COOKBOOK. I enclose $10.95 plus $1.50 shipping/handling for each copy. Washington residents add applicable sales tax. Ship book(s) to:

_____
Name

_____
Address

_____   _____   _____
City   State   Zip

Mail Form To: Columbia River Press, Box 1647, Wenatchee, WA 98801

MAIL ORDER FORM

Please send me _____ copies of THE COLUMBIA RIVER COOKBOOK. I enclose $10.95 plus $1.50 shipping/handling for each copy. Washington residents add applicable sales tax. Ship book(s) to:

_____
Name

_____
Address

_____   _____   _____
City   State   Zip

Mail Form To: Columbia River Press, Box 1647, Wenatchee, WA 98801